NEW AND REVISED

Still Higher for His Highest

Now with NIV Text

OSWALD CHAMBERS

Daybreak Books

Zondervan Publishing House
Grand Rapids, Michigan

STILL HIGHER FOR HIS HIGHEST
Copyright © 1970 by D. W. Lambert

Daybreak Books are published by
Zondervan Publishing House
1415 Lake Dr., S.E.
Grand Rapids, MI 49506

Library of Congress Cataloging-in-Publication Data

Chambers, Oswald, 1874–1917.
  Still higher for His highest : now with NIV text / by Oswald
Chambers.
    p. cm.
  ISBN 0-310-23600-2
  1. devotional calendars. I. Title.
BV4811.C4593 1989
242'.2—dc20   89-9104
                                                       CIP

Unless otherwise noted, Scripture quotations are taken from the
Holy Bible: New International Version (North American Edition),
copyright © 1973, 1978, 1984 by The International Bible Society.
Used by permission of Zondervan Bible Publishers. Scripture
quotations in textual material are taken from the King James
Version.

Printed in the United States of America

91 92 93 94 95 96 97 / EE / 10 9 8 7 6 5 4 3 2

This edition is printed on acid-free paper and meets the American
National Standards Institute Z39.48 standard.

PROLOGUE

Some forty years ago, *My Utmost for His Highest,* Daily Readings from Oswald Chambers, was published and soon became a devotional classic, known and loved by many.

Now the request has come for a further selection from the works of that remarkable spiritual teacher.

Turning over the mass of material available one is inclined to say what Dryden said of Chaucer, "Here is God's Plenty." Many of the extracts are from the B. T. C. Journal issued April 1932 and April 1952, also from O. C.'s books already in print. I am especially indebted to Miss Kathleen Chambers for the loan of some hitherto unprinted lecture notes on the Prophets.

Oswald Chambers used to speak of our Lord "presenting the Truth in nugget form"; while later the apostles "beat out the nuggets into negotiable gold." The daily readings given here may be regarded as nuggets of spiritual truth, to be turned into coinage for daily living. The process involves not only prayerful meditation, but, as our author would insist, strenuous thought and spiritual concentration.

May the Holy Spirit quicken and enlighten all who use this book.   *D. W. L.*

Can You See the Highest?

He reached down from on high and took hold of me; he drew me out of deep waters *(Psalm 18:16).*

And God raised us up with Christ and seated us with him in the heavenly realms in Christ Jesus *(Ephesians 2:6).*

T he Lord Jesus Christ is the Highest. Is there anyone else higher to you than He is? Your life is never safeguarded until Jesus is seen to be the Highest. Past experience will not keep you, neither will deliverance from sin; the only safeguarding power is The Highest. If there is a breath of confidence anywhere else, there will be disaster, and it is by the mercy of God that you are allowed to stumble, or to be pain-smitten, until you learn that He does it all—*He* keeps you from stumbling, *He* raises you up and keeps you up, *He* sends from above and delivers you. "Now unto Him that is able to keep you from falling. . . ."

Whenever there is a complication in your circumstances, do nothing until you see the Highest—not sometimes, but always (cf. Isaiah 50:10). Can you see the Lord in your thinking? If not, suspend your judgment until you can. Can you see the face of Jesus in your affections? If not, restrain them until you can. Can you see God in your circumstances? If not, do nothing until you can. Our Lord can trust anything to the man or woman who sees Him.

Are You Succoured by the Highest?

The Spirit of the Sovereign Lord is on me, because the LORD has anointed me to preach good news to the poor. He has sent me to bind up the brokenhearted, to proclaim freedom for the captives and release for the prisoners, to proclaim the year of the LORD's favor and the day of vengeance of our God, to comfort all who mourn *(Isaiah 61: 1–2)*.

If you have any encouragement from being united with Christ, if any comfort from his love, if any fellowship with the Spirit, if any tenderness and compassion, then make my joy complete by being like-minded, having the same love, being one in spirit and purpose *(Philippians 2:1–2)*.

U ntil a worker knows the succour of God, he is in danger of becoming a stumbling block to other souls. If we are not being succoured by the Highest, of what use can we be to those folks who are crushed by sorrows of which we know nothing? "The sacrifices of God are a broken heart" broken beyond any patching up, but— "He hath sent Me to bind up the broken-hearted." The heart which has been bound up and succoured by the Lord Jesus Christ will never be got on the train of self-interest, there is no selfishness left in it. "As one whom his mother comforteth, so will I comfort you." That is the most powerful thing God can do for us. The great note of the life which is comforted of God is— "For my Lord I live; by my Lord I am strengthened, and in my Lord I am succoured."

The Greatest Good Is the Highest End

"If you, then, though you are evil, know how to give good gifts to your children, how much more will your Father in heaven give good good gifts to those who ask him! In everything, do to others what you would have them do to you, for this sums up the Law and the Prophets. Enter through the narrow gate. For wide is the gate and broad is the road that leads to destruction, and many enter through it. But small is the gate and narrow the road that leads to life, and only a few find it" *(Matthew 7:11–14)*.

The Shorter Catechism states, in answer to the question, "What is man's chief end?" that "Man's chief end is to glorify God and enjoy Him for ever." It is not what man puts into his body or on his body, but what he brings out of his body (cf. Matthew 15:17–20), and what he brings out of what he puts on his body, viz., his money, that reveals what he considers his chief end. A great many people imagine they have glorified God when they have given two halfpennies for a penny, or have saved a halfpenny. The highest good to them is to keep economic relations right, the highest Good from Jesus Christ's standpoint never dawns on them. The craze to-day is that the highest good is what a man has to live on: feed him, keep his body healthy, and his moral and religious life will be all right. That is the highest good according to the standard of many. As Christians it is more important to know how to live than what to live on.

_____

The Greatest Good Is the Highest Evangel

"Not everyone who says to me, 'Lord, Lord,' will enter the kingdom of heaven, but only he who does the will of my Father who is in heaven" *(Matthew 7:21).*

T o apply the rule of the kingdom of God to our daily life is done not by our heads but by the obedience of our hearts. "If you are ever going to get the true blessedness," says Jesus, "it must be by living your life according to the rule of God." How are we going to discern the rule of God? Jesus told Nicodemus: "If you are born from above you will *see* the kingdom of God, and *enter into it*" (John 3:3, 5). Then after we have entered into the kingdom of God, are we going to apply its rule to our bodily life, our mental life, our spiritual life? We are at liberty to stop at any point, and our Lord will never cast it up at us; but think what we shall feel like when we see Him if all the "thank you" we gave Him for His unspeakable salvation was an obstinate determination to serve Him in our own way, not His.

_____

Heart in the Heavens, Feet on Earth

All of us also lived among them at one time, gratifying the cravings of our sinful nature and following its desires and thoughts. Like the rest, we were by nature objects of wrath. But because of his great love for us, God, who is rich in mercy, made us alive with Christ even when we were dead in transgressions—it is by grace you have been saved. And God raised us up with Christ and

seated us with him in the heavenly realms in Christ Jesus
(Ephesians 2:3–6).

B eing seated together in heavenly places in Christ
Jesus does not mean lolling about on the mount of
transfiguration, singing ecstatic hymns, and letting demon-
possessed boys go to the devil in the valley; it means being
in the accursed places of this earth as far as the walk of the
feet is concerned but in undisturbed communion with God.

" . . . while we look not at the things which are seen" —
that battle never stops. The things that are seen are not the
devil but the pressing things, the things that distract; when
Christ is formed in us and essential vision comes through
looking at the things which are not seen, we find that God
makes other people shadows. If my saintly friends are
images of God to me, I have much further to go yet. God
alone must be my Stay and Source and everything. That is
the way the godly life is lived.

JANUARY 6 _____

Is God Really First?

"But seek first his kingdom and his righteousness, and all
these things will be given to you as well" *(Matthew 6:33)*.

T he great curse of modern Christianity is that people
will not be careless about things they have no right to
be careful about, and they will not let God make them
careful about their relationship to Him. Sum it up for
yourself—what do you think about most, not on the
surface, but in the deep centre of your being? What is the
real basal thought of your life—"what ye shall eat, what ye
shall drink, what ye shall put on"? None of us are so stupid

9

or lacking in cunning as to say we do not think of these things: but if we think of what will happen to "all these things" if we put God first, we know where we are. If He is first you know you can never think of anything He will forget.

JANUARY 7 _____

Are We Letting God Work?

Jesus said to them, "My Father is always at his work to this very day, and I, too, am working" *(John 5:17)*.

What we have to do, and what God cannot do, is to work out what He has worked in. We try to do God's work for Him, and God has to wait until we are passive enough to let Him work in us. To believe in Jesus means retiring and letting God take the mastership inside. That is all God asks of us. Have we ever got into the way of letting God work or are we so amazingly important that we really wonder what the Almighty does before we are up in the morning! We are so certain we know what is right, and if we don't always keep at it God cannot get on. Compare that view with the grand, marvelous working of God in the life of the Lord Jesus. Our Lord did not work for God; He said, "The Father that dwelleth in Me, He doeth the works."

JANUARY 8 _____

Redemption, God's Final Purpose

For God was pleased to have all his fullness dwell in him, and through him to reconcile to himself all things, whether things on earth or things in heaven, by making

10

peace through his blood, shed on the cross *(Colossians 1:19–20).*

T he truth about God is Jesus Christ—light, life and love. Whatever is dark to us will, by means of our obedience, become as clear as the truth which we have made ours by obedience. The bit we do know is the most glorious, unfathomable delight conceivable, and that is going to be true about everything to do with God and us. The process is continual obedience.

The world is for redemption, not for progress, and a Christian is one who has been taken into that secret by the personal experience of Redemption. It is a continual revelation centring round one thing, the Cross of God in Jesus Christ, and the characteristic is that we have to be crucified too, and live only the life "hid with Christ in God."

JANUARY 9 _____

Obeying the Heavenly Vision

"So then, King Agrippa, I was not disobedient to the vision from heaven" *(Acts 26:19).*

B ut rise and stand upon thy feet: for I have appeared unto thee for this purpose, to make thee a minister and a witness both of these things which thou hast seen, and of those things in which I will appear unto thee" (Acts 26:16).

We all have visions, if we are spiritual at all, of what Jesus Christ wants. When we are born again and come into contact with Him, we know what He wants us to be, and the great thing is to learn how not to be disobedient to the vision, not say it cannot be attained. Verse 16 is immensely

11

commanding; there is nothing there apart from the personal relationship. Paul was not given a message or a doctrine, nor a direction of thought; he was brought into a vivid, personal, overmastering relationship to Jesus Christ.

Defiling the Temple

If anyone destroys God's temple, God will destroy him: for God's temple is sacred, and you are that temple (1 Corinthians 3:17).

That truth applied to us individually means this—once realize that your body is the temple of the Holy Ghost, and you can never again do with success what you once did; the slightest attempt to do so brings a painful realization of Paul's words in 1 Corinthians 3:17—"If any man destroyeth the temple of God, him shall God destroy." I have no jurisdiction over my body, there is only one honour at stake, the honour of God. Defiling the temple of the Holy Ghost is the result of my exercising my right to myself; realizing this made Paul say, "I buffet my body and bring it into bondage: lest by any means, after that I have preached to others, I myself should be rejected."

The True Work of the True Church

And to present her to himself as a radiant church, without stain or wrinkle or any other blemish, but holy and blameless (Ephesians 5:27).

Remember the height from which you have fallen! Repent and do the things you did at first. If you do not repent, I will come to you and remove your lampstand from its place *(Revelation 2:5)*.

J esus Christ has done a work we cannot do, and the manifestation of that glorious finished work is seen in every man and woman who stands on that finished work in conscious committing faith. The Church ("that which is called out") is called out to proclaim what Jesus Christ has done and can do, to stand backed by Almighty God for strong, stern, surgical, spiritual salvation and sanctification. The Church is not called to success; the Church is called to deliver God's message and to be for the praise of His glory. Her one desire is to be the fitted Bride of Christ, "without spot, or wrinkle, or any such thing." The Church must stand for the GLORY OF GOD and for what God can do—not as a socialistic institution under the patronage of God. The voice of the Lord cries again to-day—"Remember therefore from whence thou art fallen, and repent, and do the first works; or else I will come in to thee quickly and will remove thy candlestick out of its place, except thou repent."

JANUARY 12

Are We Willing to Come to Him?

"Come to me, all you who are weary and burdened, and I will give you rest" *(Matthew 11:28)*.

O ur Lord's marvelous message for all time is familiar: "Come unto Me . . . and I will give you rest." "The wayfaring men, yea fools, shall not err therein." When a

13

man does err in the way of God, it is because he is wise in his own conceits. When the facts of life have humbled us, when introspection has stripped us of our own miserable self-interest and we receive a startling diagnosis of ourselves by the Holy Spirit, we are by that painful experience brought to the place where we can hear the marvelous message—profounder than the profoundest philosophies earth ever wove, "Come unto Me, all ye that labour and are heavy laden, and I will give you rest." Until this experience comes men may patronize Jesus Christ, but they do not come to Him for salvation. The only solution is the one given by Jesus Christ Himself to a good upright man of His day: "Marvel not that I say unto thee, ye must be born from above."

The Standard, "As I Have Loved You"

> "A new command I give you: Love one another. As I have loved you, so you must love one another" *(John 13:34)*.

R emember the standard, *"as I have loved you."* I wonder where the best of us are according to that standard? How many of us have turned away over and over again in disgust at men, and when we get alone with the Lord Jesus He speaks no word, but the memory of Him is quite sufficient to bring the rebuke—"as I have loved you." It takes severe training to think habitually along the lines Jesus Christ has laid down, although we act on them impulsively at times.

The Tragedy of the Backslider

"Has not my inheritance become to me like a speckled bird of prey that other birds of prey surround and attack?" *(Jeremiah 12:9).*

I s mine heritage unto me as a speckled bird of prey?" This is not a picture of a saint living a holy life in the world; it is the picture of a saint who is leaving God and going into the world, with the result that the birds of prey, i.e., those who have never recognized God, are tearing that life to bits, and God does not protect it. That is the thing that staggered Jeremiah. God is bringing him to see the reason: the people have rebelled against Him. If I backslide, I take some of the glorious plumage of the heritage of God with me, and as it gets bedraggled I am torn to pieces by the people who never knew Jesus Christ.

"Many shepherds have destroyed my vineyard, . . . no man layeth it to heart." God would have been "a wall of fire round about and the glory in the midst" if they had been obedient. The difference between God as a consuming fire and natural fire is just this, that the further you get away from God the more fiercely you feel His burnings, but when you are close to Him, you find it is a glorious protection.

The Supernatural Lord Comes in Common Ways

Turning around, Jesus saw them following and asked, "What do you want?" They said, "Rabbi" (which means

Teacher), "where are you staying?" "Come," he replied, "and you will will see." So they went and saw where he was staying, and spent that day with him. It was about the tenth hour. Andrew, Simon Peter's brother, was one of the two who heard what John had said and who had followed Jesus *(John 1:38–40)*.

T here is something so natural and yet so supernatural about Jesus. We never read that Jesus buttonholed anybody; these men came to Him and asked, "Master, where do you live?" He said "Come, and ye shall see"— obvious and simple, yet full of Divine power. The difference between the Christianity stamped by the Holy Ghost and that stamped by ecstacy and fanaticism is just here: the one makes the supernatural "spooky" and puts the natural nowhere; the other makes the supernatural natural. Jesus does not come to men in extraordinary ways, but in the most ordinary things—washing disciples' feet; preparing breakfast; at a wedding feast. The early disciples were not attracted to Jesus because of their sense of sin; they were religious men, in touch with the elemental forces of nature, simple and unconventional, and when they saw Jesus their spirit indicated at once: "This is the very One we have been looking for."

JANUARY 16 _____

The Wonder of Faith

By faith he left Egypt, not fearing the king's anger; he persevered because he saw him who is invisible *(Hebrews 11:27)*.

16

F aith cannot be intellectually defined; faith is the inborn capacity to see God behind everything, the wonder that keeps you an eternal child. What is your faith to you—a wonderful thing, or a bandbox thing? Satisfaction is too often the peace of death; wonder is the very essence of life. Beware always of losing the wonder, and the first thing that stops wonder is religious conviction. Whenever you give a trite testimony the wonder is gone. The only evidence of salvation or sanctification is that the sense of wonder is developing, not at things as they are, but at the One who made them as they are. There is no set definition of faith into which you can fit these men and women; they were heroes of faith because they "endured, as seeing Him who is invisible."

JANUARY 17 _____

The Discipline of Love

If I speak in the tongues of men and of angels, but have not love, I am only a resounding gong or a clanging cymbal. If I have the gift of prophecy and can fathom all mysteries and all knowledge, and if I have a faith that can move mountains, but have not love, I am nothing. If I give all I possess to the poor and surrender my body to the flames, but have not love, I gain nothing. Love is patient, love is kind. It does not envy, it does not boast, it is not proud. It is not rude, it is not self-seeking, it is not easily angered, it keeps no record of wrongs. Love does not delight in evil but rejoices with the truth. It always protects, always trusts, always hopes, always perseveres. Love never fails. But where there are prophecies, they will cease; where there is knowledge, it will pass away. For we know in part and we prophesy in part, but when perfection comes, the imperfect disappears. When I was a child, I talked like a child, I thought like a child, I reasoned like a child. When I became a man, I put childish ways behind me. Now we see but a poor reflection; then we shall see face to face. Now I know in part; then I shall know fully, even as I am fully known. And now these three remain: faith, hope, and love. But the greatest of these is love *(1 Corinthians 13)*.

First Corinthians 13 is the description of how Christianity works out in a man's actual experience. Love is the sovereign preference of my person for another; my love for Jesus Christ means that I deliberately identify myself with His interests in other people—and the Lord is interested in some funny folk. Jesus Christ demands, if I am born from above and have inherited His disposition, that I show it, not to fictitious people, but to the people I live beside. Our Heavenly Father has an amazing sense of humour; He will bring across your path the kind of people who manifest to you what you have been to Him. If you have been obstinate, that is why you have got that fellow around you just now, and Jesus says, "Show him the attitude I showed you." That is experimental Christianity with no humbug. It means showing the disposition of Jesus Christ to the man who deliberately wrongs you, and it takes some doing.

JANUARY 18 _____

Spiritual Instability

He is a double-minded man, unstable in all he does *(James 1:8)*.

O ur Lord refers to this instability in His parable of the sower and the seed—"they receive the word gladly, but they have no root in themselves"—quicksilver Christians. They may have as many conversions as there are days in the year, and at the end of the year remain the same unreliable, emotional people, utterly incapable of resting in a stable point of truth, and they become eager adherents of every new interest. The main characteristic of young modern life to-day is an intense craving to be interested. Literature, amusements, all indicate this tendency, and in religion the Church is apt to pander to the demand to be intcrested; consequently men won't face the rugged facts of the Gospel because when the Holy Spirit comes in He challenges a man's will, demands a reconstruction of his whole life, and produces a change of mind which will work havoc in his former complacency.

JANUARY 19 _____

The True Prophet Identified With Sin

> At the end of seven days the word of the LORD came to me: "Son of man, I have made you a watchman for the house of Israel; so hear the word I speak and give them warning from me" *(Ezekiel 3:16–17).*

E zekiel, in common with all the Old Testament prophets, had not to generate his message out of his own individuality, he had simply to obey God. The obedient life is stated for us in Matthew 11:25 and 1 John 1:7, simplicity and single unfoldedness before God. Do I believe in God, or in a wise and understanding way of doing God's work?

The message God laid on Ezekiel to deliver found no natural affinity for itself to him; the message was built on a supernatural affinity with God. God mortifies our affinities that limit Him. Like the apostle Paul, Ezekiel has a "Woe is unto me, if I preach not the gospel"; he had a commission to warn the people of God, not win them, and he was to speak according to God's discretion, not according to his own judgment.

JANUARY 20 _____

The Failure of Mere Temperament

Then they sat on the ground with him for seven days and seven nights. No one said a word to him, because they saw how great his suffering was *(Job 2:13)*.

Temperamental—the way a man looks at life. My temperament is an inner disposition which influences my thoughts and actions to a certain extent, i.e., I am either pessimistic or optimistic according to the way my blood circulates. It is an insult to take the temperamental line in dealing with human beings—"Cheer up, look on the bright side"; there are some types of suffering before which the only thing you can do is to keep your mouth shut. There are times when a man needs to be handled by God, not by his fellow men, and part of the gift of man's wisdom is to know how to be reverent with what he does not understand.

The Disasters of Fellowship With Him

We do not want you to be uninformed, brothers, about the hardships we suffered in the province of Asia. We were under great pressure, far beyond our ability to endure, so that we despaired even of life. Indeed, in our hearts we felt the sentence of death. But this happened that we might not rely on ourselves but on God, who raises the dead *(2 Corinthians 1:8–9)*.

There are disasters to be faced by the one who is in real fellowship with the Lord Jesus Christ. God has never promised to keep us immune from trouble; He says "I will be with him in trouble," which is a very different thing. Paul was "an apostle of Jesus Christ by the will of God," and it is this fact that accounts for the crushing criticism and the spiteful treatment to which he was subjected by those who could not discern on what authority he based his apostleship. That was the ground Paul stood on, and that only—he was an apostle *"by the will of God"* (see Colossians 1:1.)

If you are experiencing the disasters of fellowship, don't get into despair, remain unswervingly and unhesitatingly faithful to the Lord Jesus Christ and refuse to compromise for one second.

Thinking About Men as Jesus Thought

"Because of the increase of wickedness, the love of most will grow cold" *(Matthew 24:12)*.

I t is easy if you are an innocent person to be shocked at immorality, but how much education in the school of Christ, how much reliance on the Holy Spirit, does it take to bring us to the place where we are shocked at pride against God?

The Spirit of God can bring us into sympathy with the work Jesus has done. "And because iniquity shall abound, the love of many shall wax cold." Jesus Christ sketched the portrait of many of us in those words twenty centuries ago. Think of the worst man or woman you ever knew—not the worst man or woman you can think of because that is vague—have you any hope for him? For her? That is the test as to whether or not you have been learning to think about men as Jesus thought of them. Does the Holy Spirit begin to convey to your mind the wonder of "that man, that woman, being 'presented perfect in Christ Jesus'"?

JANUARY 23 _____

Is Life and Conduct Right?

> "Leave your gift there in front of the altar. First go and be reconciled to your brother; then come and offer your gift" *(Matthew 5:24)*.

M any a powerless, fruitless Christian life has resulted from some insignificant thing—*"first go."* The thing that fights longest against the Spirit of God's demands is my prideful claim to my right to myself, which is the essence of sin. It is extraordinary what we are brought up against when the Spirit of God is at work in us; the only sign of regeneration in practical experience is that we begin to make our life in accordance with the principles of God. Am

I prepared to be identified with the death of Jesus morally? The Holy Spirit will drive it home—am I going to see that my goods are up to sample, that my back premises are in keeping with the shop window? Am I trying to put a snowdrift over a rubbish heap, or am I going to wash myself white in the blood of the Lamb? If I have received the Holy Spirit, I must show it; the thing must be visible all through. If Jesus Christ cannot alter a man's disposition, Christianity is a cunningly devised fable. Christianity means the manifestation of a strong family likeness to Jesus.

Why Did Jesus Offend?

> But Jesus said to them, "Only in his home town and in his own house is a prophet without honor" *(Matthew 13:57).*

H e is despised and rejected of men." Jesus offended many; His own home folk were the first to be offended. "And when His friends heard of it, they went out to lay hold on Him: for they said, He is beside Himself"— "He assumes too much for His humble position." When he preached in the synagogue, they were astonished, but—"Is not this the carpenter? . . . And they were offended at Him." The Jews were offended at Jesus because they looked for a warrior king in their coming Messiah, and the carelessness of Jesus over temporal positions and honour did not commend itself to them. The Pharisees were offended at Him because His teaching showed up the hollow emptiness of their profession. His own disciples were offended at Him—"All ye shall be offended in Me this night."

_____

Claiming All Sufficient Grace

And God is able to make all grace abound to you, so that
in all things at all times, having all that you need, you will
abound in every good work *(2 Corinthians 9:8).*

When God brings us up against difficult circumstances
that reveal the inability of our human nature it is not
that we may sink back and say, "Oh dear, I thought I
should have been all right by now"; it is that we may learn
to draw on our union with Jesus Christ and claim that we
have sufficient grace to do this particular thing according to
God's will. If we are vitally connected with God in our
thinking we shall find we can walk; but if we have not been
thinking rightly we will succumb—"I cannot do this." If we
are thinking along the line of God's grace, that He is able to
make all grace abound unto us, we will not only stand, but
walk as a son or daughter of God and prove that His grace
is sufficient. To be weak in God's strength is a crime.

_____

The Offence of the Cross and the Blood

But we preach Christ crucified: a stumbling block to Jews
and foolishness to Gentiles *(1 Corinthians 1:23).*

Blood" was, and is, the offence. "You Christians
wallow in blood," it is objected, "could no other word

be used? There is something so offensive in the word 'blood.' And why talk so much about sin? Sin is but a defect, slowly being outgrown in the evolution of man." "Blood," the vital life-stream—offensive! Is there nothing offensive in sin, that devastating thing which poisons the very fountain of life, which makes the world a howling wilderness and our cities unendurable to thought—a defect! The evolutionary idea sounds all right; it is the thinker himself who is wrong. Sin has alienated man from God and the story of the ages is an accumulation of wrongdoing and of judgment days; there is utter hopelessness in any attempt to meet the righteousness of God; but let a man begin to realize what sin is, then *"the blood of Jesus Christ His Son cleanseth us from all sin"* will be a holy word to his soul. "The Cross" and "the blood of Jesus" are indeed names for profound mysteries, but when a soul shattered by the crushing sense of his guilt believes that through the blood of Jesus there is forgiveness for sin, he receives a new life-energy; he is purged from his old sins.

JANUARY 27 _____

The Recognition of Deity

Simon Peter answered, "You are the Christ, the Son of the living God" *(Matthew 16:16).*

I mmediately you lose sight of the central, majestic figure of Jesus Christ, you are swept off your feet by all kinds of doctrine; and when big things hit us we find that our religion does not stand us in good stead; our creed does not agree with Jesus Christ.

The revelation of the Deity of Christ does not come to a

man's intellect first, but to his heart and life, and he says with amazement, "Thou art the Christ, the Son of the living God." The great point of the Bible revelation of God is not only that God was in Christ but that Jesus Christ is God. "He that hath seen Me hath seen the Father," said Jesus. If Jesus Christ is not God, then the only God we have is an abstraction of our own minds.

JANUARY 28 _____

Stablished by Faith That Receives

So then, just as you received Christ Jesus as Lord, continue to live in him, rooted and built up in him, strengthened in the faith as you were taught, and overflowing with thankfulness *(Colossians 2:6–7)*.

A nd stablished by your faith." Think of the things you are trying to have faith for! Stop thinking of them and think about your state in God through receiving Christ Jesus; see how God has enabled you to walk where you used to totter, and see what marvelous strength you have in Him. "I can do all things in Him that strengthened me," says Paul. Is that mere poetry or a fact? Paul never talked poetry only. All the great blessings of God in salvation and sanctification, all the Holy Spirit's illumination, are ours not because we obey; they are ours because we have put ourselves into a right relationship with God by receiving Christ Jesus, and we obey spontaneously. As we look back we find that every time we have been blessed it was not through mechanical obedience, but by receiving from Jesus something that enabled us to obey without knowing it, and life was flooded with the power of God. We make it hard

26

for people—Do this and that, and they obey and nothing happens. We have left out altogether the receiving of Christ Jesus the Lord; we have to be rooted and built up in Him.

"Eating" at God's Command

> And he said to me, "Son of man, eat what is before you, eat this scroll; then go and speak to the house of Israel." So I opened my mouth, and he gave me the scroll to eat. Then he said to me, "Son of man, eat this scroll I am giving you and fill your stomach with it." So I ate it, and it tasted as sweet as honey in my mouth *(Ezekiel 3:1—3)*.

The conception of "swallowing" a word of God has in it the essence of obedience. There is no room for debate when God speaks. Obedience is never the outcome of intellectual discernment; it springs from moral simplicity, keeping in the light of God. "Eat this roll"—an unpalatable thing to do, but Ezekiel obeyed, "and it was in my mouth as honey for sweetness." Obedience to a word of God always brings an amazing sweetness to the life of the obeyer. Over and over again God brings up to a word of His, e.g., the condition of discipleship (Luke 14:26), and we say, "Oh, I couldn't possibly 'swallow' that," and we nibble at it and run away from it, and God brings us back to it again and again until we are willing to obey; immediately we obey and appropriate the word it becomes "as honey for sweetness."

Our Civilization and Christ's Call

"But seek first his kingdom and his righteousness, and all
these things will be given to you as well" *(Matthew 6:33).*

T o follow Jesus Christ to-day is to follow a madman
according to the ideals of present-day civilization. We
have made a thousand and one necessities until our system
of civilized life is as cast iron, and then we apologize to the
Lord for not following Him. "God can never mean that I
have to follow Him at the cost of all I have?" But He does
mean it. Instantly the clash is between our civilization and
the call of Jesus Christ. Read the Sermon on the Mount—
"Seek ye first the kingdom of God"—and apply it to
modern life and you will find its statements are either those
of a madman or of God Incarnate.

Unbelief Hinders God's Work

And he did not do many miracles there because of their
lack of faith *(Matthew 13:58).*

T he basis of human life is not rational, but redemptive;
consequently it ought to be an easy thing for the
Christian who thinks to conceive of any and every type of
man being presented perfect in Christ Jesus. But how
seldom we do think! If I am an earnest evangelical preacher
I may say to a man, "Oh yes, God can save you," while in
my own heart I don't believe there is much hope for him.
Our unbelief stands as the supreme barrier to Christ's work
in men's souls. "And He did not many mighty works there

because of their unbelief." Once let me get over my own
slowness of heart to believe in Jesus Christ's power to save
and I become a real generator of His power to men.
"Neither is there salvation in any other; for there is none
other name under heaven given among men, whereby we
must be saved."

Regeneration

> Through these he has given us his very great and
> precious promises, so that through them you may
> participate in the divine nature and escape the corruption
> in the world caused by evil desires *(2 Peter 1:4)*.

All through the Bible the authority of God's law is
unflinchingly revealed; but along with man's responsibility to meet that demand comes the revelation of
Regeneration, viz., that we can be regenerated into a life in
which the holiness that is given to us, not the power to
imitate His holiness, but the very nature of God is imparted
to us. We are "presenced with divinity"; "made partakers
of the divine nature." God becomes incarnated in us
through the Redemption. The Bible reveals that Jesus
Christ, Who was God Incarnate, has lifted the whole human
race on to another plane of responsibility; and on that plane
our responsibility does not lie in being absolutely holy, but
in seeing that we allow God to be absolutely holy in us.

Wearing Saul's Armour

> Then Saul dressed David in his own tunic. He put a coat
> of armour on him and a bronze helmet on his head.
> David fastened on his sword over the tunic and tried
> walking around, because he was not used to them
> (1 Samuel 17:38–39).

I f your religion injures your intelligence, it is bad; if it
injures your character, it is vicious; if it injures your
conscience, it is criminal." (Amiel.)

Therefore don't try and wear Saul's armour. It is pathetic
to see us when we are about a month old in grace trying to
wear the terrific armour of mature saints; we go about
clanking great sentiments on profound themes while our
practical life laughs at us. If we obey God, He will introduce
us by the current of events and by our obedience into the
place where these truths become real to us, and we begin to
"grow up into Him in all things." Anything that relieves us
from personal accountability to Jesus Christ is corrupt.

Discipline of the Body

> No, I beat my body and make it my slave so that after I
> have preached to others, I myself will not be disqualified
> for the prize (1 Corinthians 9:27).

T he forming of new habits is difficult until you get into
the way of doing it, then everything you meet with
aids you in developing along the right line. It is good
practice to sit down for five minutes and do nothing; in that

way you will soon discover how little control you have over yourself. In forming a new habit it is vitally important to insist on bringing the body under control first. Paul says, "I maul and master my body, in case, after preaching to others, I am disqualified myself." The natural man is created by God as well as the new man in Christ, and the new man has to be manifested by the natural man in his mortal flesh.

FEBRUARY 4 _____

Discipline of the Mind

Let your gentleness be evident to all. The Lord is near (Philippians 4:5).

Our thinking processes are largely subject to the law of habit. "Let your forbearance," i.e., self-control, "be made known unto all men." Self-control is nothing more than a mental habit which controls the body and mind by a dominant relationship, viz., the immediate presence of the Lord—"for the Lord is at hand." The danger in spiritual matters is that we do not *think* godliness; we let ideas and conceptions of godliness lift us up at times, but we do not form the habit of godly thinking. Thinking godliness cannot be done in spurts, it is a steady habitual trend. God does not give us our physical or mental habits; He gives us the power to form any kind of habits we like, and in the spiritual domain we have to form the habit of godly thinking.

Meditate on These Things

> Be diligent in these matters; give yourself wholly to them,
> so that everyone may see your progress (1 Timothy
> 4:15).

M editate upon these things." Meditation means getting to the middle of a thing, pinning yourself down to a certain thing, and concentratedly brooding upon it. The majority of us attend only to the "muddle" of things; consequently we get spiritual indigestion, the counterpart of physical indigestion, a desperately gloomy state of affairs. We cannot see anything rightly, and all we do see is stars. "Faith is the evidence of things not seen." Suppose Jesus suddenly lifted the veil from our eyes and let us see angels ministering to us, His own presence with us, the Holy Ghost in us, and the Father around us; how amazed we should be! We have lived in the "muddle" instead of in the middle of things. Faith gets us into the middle, which is God and God's purpose. "Lord, I pray Thee, open his eyes, that he may see;" and when his eyes were opened he saw the hosts of God and nothing else (2 Kings 6:17).

Deliverance From Misunderstanding

> Yet I am always with you; you hold me by my right
> hand. You guide me with your counsel, and afterward
> you will take me into glory. Whom have I in heaven but
> you? And being with you, I desire nothing on earth"
> (Psalm 73:23–25).

The first thing a Christian is emancipated from is the tyranny of moods and the tyranny of feeling he is not understood. These things are the most fruitful sources of misery. Half the misery in the world comes because one person demands of another a complete understanding, which is absolutely impossible. The only Being Who understands us is the Being Who made us. It is a tremendous emancipation to get rid of every kind of self-consideration and learn to heed only one thing, the relationship between God and ourselves. "In all the world there is none but thee, my God, there is none but thee." Once we get there, other people become shadows, beautiful shadows, but shadows under God's control.

Prayer, an Effort of the Will

"If you remain in me and my words remain in you, ask whatever you wish, and it will be given you" *(John 15:7).*

Enter into thy closet, and when thou hast shut thy door, pray to thy Father which is in secret." Prayer that is not an effort of the will is unrecognized by God. "Ye shall ask what ye *will,*" said Jesus. That does not mean ask anything you like, but what you *will.* What are you actively willing? Ask for that. We shall find that we *ask* very few things. The tendency in prayer to leave ourselves all abroad to the influence of a meeting or a special season is not scriptural. Prayer is an effort of will, and Jesus Christ instructs us by using the word *ask.* "Everyone that asketh receiveth." These words are an amazing revelation of the simplicity with which God would have us pray.

Neglect Not the Gift

Do not neglect your gift, which was given you through a prophetic message when the body of elders laid their hands on you *(1 Timothy 4:14)*.

N eglect not the gift that is in thee." We have to be careful not to neglect the spiritual reality planted in us by God. The first thing that contact with reality does is to enable us to diagnose our moods. It is a great moment when we realize that we have the power to trample on certain moods. Moods never go by praying, moods go by kicking. A mood nearly always has its seat in the physical condition, not in the moral, and it is a continual effort to refuse to listen to those moods which arise from a physical condition; we must not submit to them for a second. It is a great thing to have something to neglect in your life, a great thing for your moral character to have something to snub. "The expulsive power of a new affection"—that is what Christianity supplies. The Spirit of God on the basis of Redemption gives us something else to think about. Are we going to think about it?

Where Do You Live?

He who dwells in the shelter of the Most High will rest in the shadow of the Almighty *(Psalm 91:1)*.

No one can tell you where the shadow of the Almighty is; you must find that out for yourself. When you have found out where it is, stay there; under that shadow no evil can ever befall you. The intensity of the moments spent under the shadow of the Almighty is the measure of your usefulness as a worker. Intensity of communion is not in feelings or emotions or in special places, but in quiet, fixed, confident centering on God. Never allow anything to hinder you from being in the place where your spiritual life is maintained.

FEBRUARY 10 ───────────────────────────

Sent of God

> And how can they preach unless they are sent? As it is written, "How beautiful are the feet of those who bring good news!" *(Romans 10:15).*

The Christian worker must be sent; he must not elect to go. Nowadays that is the last thing thought of; it is a determination on the part of the individual: This is something I can do and I am going to do it. Beware of demanding that people go into work; it is a craze; the majority of saved souls are not fit to feed themselves yet. How am I to know I have been sent of God? First, by the realization that I am utterly weak and powerless and if I am to be of any use to God, God must do it all the time. Is this the humiliating certainty of my soul, or merely a sentimental phrase? Second, because I know I have to point men to Jesus Christ, not get them to think what a holy man I am. The only way to be sent is to let God lift us right out of any sense of fitness in ourselves and place us where He will.

35

Discerning Through Doing

"If any one chooses to do God's will, he will find out whether my teaching comes from God or whether I speak on my own" *(John 7:17)*.

J esus says we shall know, i.e., discern, whether His teaching is of God or not when we do what we know to be His Will. We discern according to our disposition. There are moments in life when the little thing matters more than anything else, times when a critical situation depends upon our attitude of mind to another person. If a man is hesitating between obeying and not obeying God, the tiniest thing contrary to obedience is quite sufficient to swing the pendulum right away from the discernment of Jesus Christ and of God. "If thou bring thy gift to the altar, and there rememberest that thy brother hath ought against thee . . . *first go."* Distempers of mind make all the difference in the discernment of Jesus Christ's teaching. Have I a distempered view about any man or woman on earth? If I have, there is a great deal of Jesus Christ's teaching I do not want to listen to; then I will never discern His teaching.

God's Final Word

Jesus replied, "Blessed are you, Simon son of Jonah, for this was not revealed to you by man, but by my Father in heaven. And I tell you that you are Peter, and on this rock I will build my church, and the gates of Hades will not overcome it" *(Matthew 16:17–18)*.

O ur Lord's teaching is God-breathed. What makes the difference between the attitude of a spiritual Christian to the teaching of Jesus and that of an unspiritual person? An unspiritual person takes the statements of Jesus to pieces as he would any man's; he dissolves Him by analysis (I John 4:3). A spiritual Christian never does. The basis of membership of the early Church was discernment of Who Jesus is by the revelation of God (Matthew 16:17–18). All through that is the test—Do I know Who Jesus Christ is, and do I know that His teaching is of God?

The mystery of the Bible is that its inspiration was direct from God (2 Peter 1:21). To believe Our Lord's consciousness about Himself commits me to accept Him as God's last endless Word. That does not mean that God is not still speaking, but it does mean that He is saying nothing different from the Final Word, Jesus Christ. All God says expounds that Word.

FEBRUARY 13 _____

Supremacy Over Our Enemies

I pursued my enemies and overtook them; I did not turn back till they were destroyed. I crushed them so that they could not rise; they fell beneath my feet. You armed me with strength for battle; you made my adversaries bow at my feet. You made my enemies turn their backs in flight, and I destroyed my foes *(Psalm 18:37–40)*.

T he supremacy over our old enemies is accounted for by the fact that God makes them our subjects. What were your enemies? Stodginess of head, laziness of body or spirit, the whole vocabulary of "I can'ts." When you live in the right place these things are made your subjects. The things that used to hinder your life with God become subject to you by His power. The very things that used to upset you now minister to you in an extraordinary way by reason of the spiritual supremacy God gives you over them. The life of a saint reveals a quietness at the heart of things; there is something firm and dependable, because the Lord is the strength of the life.

FEBRUARY 14

God in the Unconscious

In the same way, the Spirit helps us in our weakness. We do not know what we ought to pray, but the Spirit himself intercedes for us with groans that words cannot express. And he who searches our hearts knows the mind of the Spirit, because the Spirit intercedes for the saints in accordance with God's will *(Romans 8: 26–27)*.

T he first moment of thinking alters our life. If for one moment we have discerned the truth, we can never be the same again. We may ignore it, or forget it, but it will not forget us. Truth once discerned goes down into the subconscious mind, but it will jump up in a most awkward way when we don't want it to. In the matter of intercession, when we pray for another, the Spirit of God works in the unconscious domain of that one's being about which we know nothing, and about which the one we pray for knows nothing; and after a while the conscious life of the one prayed for begins to show signs of softening and unrest, of enquiry and a desire to know something. It seems stupid to think that if we pray for all that will happen, but remember to Whom we pray. We pray to a God Who understands the unconscious depths of a man's personality, and He has told us to pray.

_____

The World and the Church

And to present her to himself as a radiant church, without stain or wrinkle or any other blemish, but holy and blameless *(Ephesians 5:27)*.

We know that we are children of God, and that the whole world is under the control of the evil one *(1 John 5:19)*.

T he Church confronts the world with a message the world craves for but resents because it comes through the Cross of Christ. The central keystone for all Time and Eternity on which the whole purpose of God depends is the Cross (Gal 6:14). When the world gets in a bad way, she refers to the Church; when prosperous, she hates it. If men could blot out the standard of the Christian Church they would do it; but in a crisis they find a need in their own heart. As preachers we are privileged by God to stand steadfast against any element that lowers His standard. We are called upon to confront the world with the Gospel of Christ, not to start off on side tracks of our own. The Church owns a mastery the world can neither ignore nor do without, the mastery of the Lord Jesus Christ.

The Witness of the Preacher

"He must become greater; I must become less" *(John 3:30)*.

A preacher must remember that his calling is different from every other calling in life; his personality has to be submerged in his message (cf. John 3:30). An orator has to work *with* men and enthuse them; a New Testament preacher has to come *upon* men with a message they resent and will not listen to at first. The Gospel comes in with a backing of Divine authority and an arrestment that men resent. There is something in every man that resents the interference of God. Before a man can be saved, the central citadel of his being has to be stormed and taken possession of by the Holy Spirit. It is easy to tell men they must be saved and filled with the Holy Ghost; but we have to live amongst men and show them what a life filled with the Holy Ghost ought to be. A preacher has to come upon men with a message and testimony that go together. The great pattern for every witness is the abiding Witness, the Lord Jesus Christ.

When He Is Come . . .

"But when he, the Spirit of truth, comes, he will guide you into all truth. He will not speak on his own; he will speak only what he hears, and he will tell you what is yet to come. He will bring glory to me by taking from what is mine and making it known to you" *(John 16:13–14)*.

T here are some things that are without meaning for us. For instance, to be told that God will give us the Holy Spirit if we ask Him, is a dead proposition; but when we come in contact with a person filled with the Spirit of God we instantly awaken to a want. Or again, if you tell half a dozen, clean-living, upright, sterling men that God so loved them that He gave His Son to die for them, only their good breeding will keep them from being amused—Why should Jesus Christ die for me? It is not a living proposition to them, not in the sphere of their life at all. Their morality is well within their own grasp; they are clean living and upright, all that can be desired; they will never be awakened in that way; but present them with Jesus Christ, or with a life that is like His life, and instantly there will awaken in them a want they were not conscious of before.

FEBRUARY 18 _____

The Snare of the Sentimentalist

As they were walking along the road, a man said to him, "I will follow you wherever you go" *(Luke 9:57)*.

Jesus replied, "No one who puts his hand to the plow and looks back is fit for service in the kingdom of God" *(Luke 9:62)*.

L ord I will follow Thee, but . . ." The wish ought to be followed by immediate obedience. I must take the wish and translate it into resolution and then into action. If I do not, the wish will translate itself into a corrupting instead of a redeeming power in my life. This principle holds good in the matter of emotions. A sentimentalist is one who delights to have high and devout emotions stirred whilst reading in an armchair or when in a prayer meeting, but he never translates his emotions into action. Consequently a sentimentalist is usually callous, self-centered, and selfish, because the emotions he likes to have stirred do not cost him anything; and when he comes across the same things in the domain where things are real and not sentimental, the revenge comes along the line of selfishness and meanness, which is always the aftermath of an unfulfilled emotion.

FEBRUARY 19 _____

Ownership

Do you not know that your body is a temple of the Holy Spirit, who is in you, whom you have received from God? You are not your own *(1 Corinthians 6:19)*.

T he instinct of ownership is seen from the first of life to the last. As soon as an infant tongue can say anything, it will say "me" and "mine." "Is this mine?" "Yes," then expect to see it smashed. The child wishes you to understand that he can do what he likes with his own. It is only the discipline of life that teaches us to keep things. The instinct of ownership is a right one, though the disposition expressed through it may be wrong. In a saint the idea of ownership is that we have the power to "glorify God by good works." What we own is the honor of Jesus Christ. Have I ever realized that His honor is at stake in my bodily life? "What? Know ye not that your body is the temple of the Holy Ghost which is in you?" Do I own my body for that one purpose? My brain to think God's thoughts after Him? We have to be intensely and personally God's.

FEBRUARY 20 _____

Our Victory Through His

"I have told you these things, so that in me you may have peace. In this world you will have trouble. But take heart! I have overcome the world" *(John 16:33)*.

I am only healthy according to the fighting corpuscles in my blood. When the fighting millions inside get low, I become diseased and after a while I shall be snuffed out. Morally it is the same; we are not born moral, we are born innocent and ignorant; morality is the outcome of fight. Immediately I am lazy in moral matters, I become immoral. Spiritually it is the same. "In the world ye shall have tribulation" i.e., everything that is not spiritual makes for our undoing; but, "be of good cheer, I have overcome the world." Why did not Our Lord say that He would help us to overcome? Because we have to imitate Him through the power He has put in us. Think of sitting in a corner before the Almighty and saying, "But my difficulties are so enormous." Thank God they are! The bigger the difficulty, the more amazing is your profit to Jesus Christ as you draw on His supernatural grace.

FEBRUARY 21 _____

Prayer and Labour

"Ask the Lord of the harvest, therefore, to send out workers into his harvest field" *(Matthew 9:38)*.

P ray ye therefore the Lord of the harvest, that He send forth labourers into His harvest." Mark the significance of the term "labour." We refuse to pray unless we get thrills. May God save us from that counterfeit of true prayer; it is the intensest form of spiritual selfishness. We have to *labour,* and to labour along the line of His direction. Jesus Christ says—*Pray.* It looks stupid; but when we labour at prayer, results happen all the time from His standpoint, because God creates something in answer to, and by means of prayer, that was not in existence before. "Labour." It is the one thing we will not do. We will take open-air meetings, we will preach—but labour at prayer! There is nothing thrilling about a labouring man's work, but it is the labouring man who makes the conceptions of the genius possible; and it is the labouring saint who makes the conceptions of his Master possible.

_____

The Prayers of the Saints

And when he had taken it, the four living creatures and twenty-four elders fell down before the Lamb. Each one had a harp and they were holding golden bowls full of incense, which are the prayers of the saints *(Revelation 5:8).*

A re we adding to the prayers of the saints or becoming sulky with God if He does not give us what we want, so taken up with the "nobility of man" that we forget what our calling is as saints? As saints we are called to go through the heroism of what we believe, not of stating what we believe, but of standing by it when the facts are dead against God. It is easy to say "God is love" when all is going well, but face a woman who has gone through bereavement and see if you find it easy to say it. There is suffering which staggers your mind as you watch it, and yet those who go through it are sustained in a way we do not understand. All day lives are passing by us; how much of the silence of heaven have we broken up by our prayers for them?

FEBRUARY 23 _____

Why Give Things Up?

Then God said, "Take your son, your only son Isaac, whom you love, and go to the region of Moriah. Sacrifice him there as a burnt offering on one of the mountains I will tell you about" *(Genesis 22:2).*

Therefore, I urge you, brothers, in view of God's mercy, to offer your bodies as living sacrifices, holy and pleasing to God—which is your spiritual worship *(Romans 12:1).*

A braham is taught by God by the ancient ritual what Paul clearly expressed in Romans 12:1. Many of us think that God wants us to give up things. God purified Abraham from this blunder, and the same discipline goes on in our lives. "Oh, well, I expect God will ask me to give that up." God nowhere tells us to give up things for the sake of giving them up. He tells us to give them up for the sake of the only thing worth having, viz., life with Himself. It is a question of loosening the bands that hinder our lives, and immediately those bands are loosened by identification with the death of Jesus, we enter into a relationship with God whereby we sacrifice our life to God. To give God my life for death is of no value; what is of value is to let Him

45

have all my powers that have been saved and sanctified, so that as Jesus sacrificed His life for His Father, I can sacrifice my life for Him. "Present your bodies a *living* sacrifice," says Paul.

Faith Triumphant

But the angel of the LORD called out to him from heaven, "Abraham! Abraham!" "Here I am," he replied. "Do not lay a hand on the boy," he said. "Do not do anything to him. Now I know that you fear God, because you have not withheld from me your son, your only son" (*Genesis 22:11–12*).

The great point of Abraham's faith in God was that he was prepared to do anything for God. Mark the difference between that and doing anything to *prove* your love to God. Abraham was there to obey God, no matter to what he went contrary. Abraham was not a pledged devotee of his own convictions, or he would have slain his son and said the voice of the angel was the voice of the devil. There is always the point of giving up convictions and traditional beliefs. If I will remain true to God, He will lead me straight through the ordeal into the inner chamber of a better knowledge of God. Our Lord taught us to pray "lead us not into temptation." Don't ask God to test you. Don't declare as Peter did, I will do anything, I will go to death for You. Abraham did not make any such declaration; he remained true to God, and God purified his faith.

FEBRUARY 25 _____

Hide in His Pavilion

The LORD is my light and my salvation—whom shall I
fear? The LORD is the stronghold of my life—of whom
shall I be afraid? *(Psalm 27:1).*

For in the day of trouble he will keep me safe in his
dwelling; he will hide me in the shelter of his tabernacle
and set me high upon a rock *(Psalm 27:5).*

God gives us the energy of an impregnable position,
viz., the heavenly places in Christ Jesus, and we have
to make the effort to be strong from that position. We have
not to work up to that position, but to work *from* it with the
full energy of will. It is impossible to live according to Our
Lord's teaching without this secret of position. We do not
get to the heavenly places by struggling, or aspiring, or
consecration; God lifts us there, and if we will work from
that position, He keeps us in His pavilion. No wonder the
life of a saint appears such an unmitigated puzzle to rational
human beings without the Spirit of God. It seems so
ridiculous and so conceited to say that God Almighty is my
Father and that He is looking after my affairs; but looked at
from the position in which Jesus places us we find it is a
marvelous revelation of truth.

FEBRUARY 26 _____

"Set Upon a Rock"

For in the day of trouble he will keep me safe in his
dwelling; he will hide me in the shelter of his tabernacle
and set me high upon a rock. Then my head will be

exalted above the enemies who surround me; at his tabernacle will I sacrifice with shouts of joy; I will sing and make music to the LORD *(Psalm 27: 5–6).*

I n our spiritual life God does not provide pinnacles on which we stand like spiritual acrobats; He provides tablelands of easy and delightful security. Recall the conception you had of holiness before you stood where you do to-day by the grace of God. It was the conception of a breathless standing on a pinnacle for a second at a time, but never with the thought of being able to live there. But when the Holy Spirit brought you there, you found it was not a pinnacle, but a plateau, a broad way, where the provision of strength and peace comes all the time, a place where it is much easier to live than lower down.

FEBRUARY 27

A Living Proposition

Therefore, just as sin entered the world through one man, and death through sin, and in this way death came to all men, because all sinned *(Romans 5:12).*

B y one man sin entered into the world. . . .'' The proposition that appeals to a healthy once-born man is that of self-realization—I want to develop myself. If you bring before him the proposition that he should be saved and give up his right to himself to Jesus Christ, it will be a dead proposition without meaning for him; but let conviction of sin, or disaster, or bereavement, or any of the great surprises of God touch him, and instantly the proposition takes on a totally new aspect and he will want to act on it. Jesus Christ always puts the emphasis on the effort of

48

obedience; there must be a live quest of the will. "If you want to know My doctrine, i.e., whether it is of God or from Myself, *do My will*," says Jesus. The truth of God is only revealed to us by obedience.

FEBRUARY 28 _____

The Cost of Cross-bearing

"A student is not above his teacher, nor a servant above his master" *(Matthew 10:24)*.

J esus tells the disciples that they will be opposed not only in private life, but that the powers of state will oppose them and they will have to suffer persecution, and some even crucifixion. Do not say—But that was simply meant for those days. If you stand true to Jesus you will find that the world will react against you with a butt, not with a caress, annoyed and antagonistic (cf. John 15:18–20).

When Our Lord spoke of the cross His disciples were to bear, He did not say that if they bore it they would become holy; He said the cross was to be borne for His sake, not for theirs. He also said that they would suffer in the same way as the prophet (Matt. 5:11–12); they suffered because of the messages they spoke from God. The tendency to-day is to say—Live a holy life, but don't talk about it; don't give your testimony; don't confess your allegiance to Jesus, and you will be left alone.

The True Life of Faith

By faith Abraham, when called to go to a place he would later receive as his inheritance, obeyed and went, even though he did not know where he was going *(Hebrews 11:8)*.

I t is not what a man achieves but what he believes and strives for that makes him noble and great. Hebrews 11 impresses this aspect of the life of faith over against the life of human perfection. The first thing faith in God does is to remove all thought of relevant perfection. Some lives may seem humanly perfect and yet not be relevant to God and His purpose. The effect such lives leave is not of a reach that exceeds its grasp, but of a completed little circle of their own. It takes a man completely severed from God to be perfect in that way. There is a difference between a perfect human life lived on earth and a personal life with God lived on earth; the former grasps that for which it reaches, the latter is grasped by that which it never can reach. The former chains us to earth by its very completeness; the latter causes us to fling ourselves unperplexed on God. The difference is not a question of sin, but the paradox of the incomplete perfection of a right relationship to God.

MARCH 1 _____

Enlarge Your Thinking

Finally, brothers, whatever is true, whatever is noble, whatever is right, whatever is pure, whatever is lovely, whatever is admirable—if anything is excellent or praise-worthy—think about such things *(Philippians 4:8)*.

We are apt to discard the virtues of those who do not know Jesus Christ and call them pagan virtues. Paul says—If there is any virtue anywhere in the world, think about it, because the natural virtues are remnants of God's handiwork and will lead to the one central Source, Jesus Christ. We have to form the habit of keeping our mental life on the line of the great and beautiful things Paul mentions. It is not a prescribed ground. It is we who make limitations and then blame God for them. Many of us behave like ostriches; we put our heads in the sand and forget altogether about the world outside— "I have had this and that experience and I am not going to think of anything else." After a while we have aches and pains in the greater part of ourselves which is outside our heads, and then we find that God sanctifies every bit of us, spirit, soul, and body. God grant we may get out into the larger horizons of God's Book.

MARCH 2

The Goal of Perfection

"Be perfect, therefore, as your heavenly Father is perfect"*(Matthew 5:48)*.

Our Lord builds His deepest teaching on the instinct of emulation. When His Spirit comes in He makes me desire not to be inferior to Him Who called me. Our example is not a good man, not even a good Christian man, but God Himself. By the grace of God I have to emulate my Father in heaven. "Be ye therefore perfect,

51

even as your Father which is in heaven is perfect" (Matt. 5:48). The most natural instinct of the supernatural life of God within me is to be worthy of my Father. To say that the doctrine of sanctification is unnatural is not true; the doctrine is based on the way God has made us. When we are born again we become natural for the first time; as long as we are in sin we are abnormal, because sin is not normal.

MARCH 3 _____

Faithful Steward: Devoted Disciple

And I bowed down and worshiped the LORD, the God of my master Abraham, who had led me on the right road to get the granddaughter of my master's brother for his son *(Genesis 24:48).*

Now it is required that those who have been given a trust must prove faithful *(1 Corinthians 4:2).*

E liezer in many respects stands as a picture of a disciple of the Lord, because the whole moulding of his life is his devotion to another, not to a sense of right or duty, but to his master (cf. John 13:13–14). We know very little about devotion to Jesus Christ. We know devotion to right and to duty, but none of that is saintly; it is purely natural. The Sermon on the Mount nowhere tells us what our duty is; it tells us the things a saint will do—the things that are not his duty, e.g., Matt. 5:39–42. Be renewed in the spirit of your mind, says Paul, not that you may do your duty, but that you may make out what God's will is.

All the reward Eliezer seeks is the happiness of his master; self-remembrance in him is dead. He is shrewd and practical yet as guileless as a child, the exact embodiment of

1 Corinthians 4:2— "It is required in stewards, that a man be found *faithful."*

MARCH 4 _____

Providence Recognized

So they called Rebekah and asked her, "Will you go with this man?" "I will go," she said *(Genesis 24:58).*

R ebekah's brother and father recognize God's hand in the whole matter (v. 50), and Rebekah's consent is sought only on the point of departure. "And she said, 'I will go.'" Those words are the answer to Eliezer's prayer. Rebekah felt the thrill which always passes through any pure young heart in the presence of a saint. A soul's trust in a saint in the providence of God is something more precious even than love. Few of us know anything about it because we are too sordidly selfish; we want things for ourselves all the time. Eliezer had only one conception, loyalty to his master, and in the providence of God he brought Rebekah straight to Isaac. This marriage, like all true marriages, concerns the Kingdom of God.

MARCH 5 _____

Glorifying God in the Everyday

"In the same way, let your light shine before men, that they may see your good deeds and praise your Father in heaven" *(Matthew 5:16).*

T he wonder of the Incarnation slips into the Life of ordinary childhood; the marvel of the Transfiguration descends to the valley and the demon-possessed boy, and the glory of the Resurrection merges into Our Lord providing breakfast for His disciples on the sea shore in the early dawn. The tendency in early Christian experience is to look for the marvellous. We are apt to mistake the sense of the heroic for being heroes. It is one thing to go through a crisis grandly, but a different thing to go through every day glorifying God when there is no witness, no limelight, and no paying the remotest attention to you. If we don't want medieval haloes, we want something that will make people say—What a wonderful man of prayer he is! What a pious, devoted woman she is! If anyone says that of you, you have not been loyal to God.

MARCH 6 _____

The Work of the God-Man

> The Word became flesh and lived for a while among us. We have seen his glory, the glory of the one and only Son, who came from the Father, full of grace and truth *(John 1:14)*.

Jesus Christ was not a Being who became Divine; He was the Godhead Incarnated. He emptied Himself of His glory in becoming Incarnate. Never separate the Incarnation from the Atonement. The Incarnation was not meant to enable God to realize Himself, but that man might realize God and gain readjustment to Him. Jesus Christ became Man for one purpose—that He might put away sin and bring the whole human race back into the oneness of identification. Jesus Christ is not an individual iota of a man; He is the whole of the human race centered before God in

54

one Person: He is God and Man in one. Man is lifted up to God in Christ, and God is brought down to man in Christ. Jesus Christ nowhere said—He that hath seen *man* hath seen the Father; but He did say that God was manifest in human flesh in His own Person that He might become the generating center for the same manifestation in every human being, and the place of His travail pangs is the Incarnation, Calvary, and the Resurrection.

MARCH 7

Revelation Through Obedience

> "I swear by myself, declares the LORD, that because you have done this and have not withheld your son, your only son, I will surely bless you and make your descendants as numerous as the stars in the sky and as the sand on the seashore. Your descendants will take possession of the cities of their enemies, and through your offspring all nations on earth will be blessed, because you have obeyed me" *(Genesis 22:16–18)*.

T he promise of God stands in relation to Abraham's tried and willing obedience. The revelation of God to me is determined by my character, not by God's (Psalm 18:25–26). If I am mean, that is how God will appear to me. "Tis because I am mean, Thy ways so oft look mean to me." But by the discipline of obedience I come to the place Abraham reached and see God as He is. The promises of God are of no use to me until by obedience I understand the nature of God. We read some things in the Bible 365 times and they mean nothing to us; then all of a sudden we see what they mean, because in some particular we have obeyed God, and instantly His character is revealed. "For how many soever be the promises of God, in Him is the yea." The "yea" must be born of obedience; when by the obedience of our life, we say "Amen," "So let it be," to a promise, then that promise is ours.

MARCH 8 _____

Blessing Through Sacrifice

Altogether, Abraham lived a hundred and seventy-five years. Then Abraham breathed his last and died at a good old age, an old man and full of years; and he was gathered to his people *(Genesis 25:7–8)*.

T he more we have to sacrifice for God, the more glorious is the reward presently. We have no right to choose our sacrifice; God will let us see where the sacrifice is to come, and it will always be on the line of what God has given you, your "Isaac," and yet His call is to sacrifice it. God is always at work on the principle of lifting up the natural and making it and the spiritual one, and very few of us will go through with it. We will cling to the natural when God wants to put a sword through it. If you go through the transfiguration of the natural you will receive it back on a new plane altogether. God wants to make eternally our own what we only possessed intermittently.

MARCH 9 _____

The Cost of Christ-following

"In the same way, any of you who does not give up everything he has cannot be my disciple" *(Luke 14:33)*.

o follow Jesus Christ to-day is to follow a madman according to the ideals of present day civilization. We have the idea that our civilization is God-ordained; but it has been built up by ourselves. We have made a thousand and one necessities until our system of civilized life is as cast iron, and then we apologize to the Lord for not following Him. "God can never mean that I have to follow Him at the cost of all I have?" But He does mean it. Instantly the clash is between our civilization and the call of Jesus Christ. Read the Sermon on the Mount—"Seek ye first the kingdom of God . . ." and apply it to modern life, and you will find its statements are either those of a madman or of God Incarnate.

Alone With the Divine Teacher

He did not say anything to them without using a parable. But when he was alone with his own disciples, he explained everything *(Mark 4:34)*.

"But when he, the Spirit of truth, comes, he will guide you into all truth. He will not speak on his own; he will speak only what he hears, and he will tell you what is yet to come. He will bring glory to me by taking from what is mine and making it known to you" *(John 16:13–14)*.

ave you ever been alone with Jesus? The disciples enjoyed the inestimable privilege not only of hearing the truth from Our Lord's own lips, but of questioning Him in secret about everything He said. We go to John Wesley, or to Adam Clarke, or to some other commentator instead of going to Jesus Himself. How can we go to Him? The

Holy Spirit is the Exponent of Jesus Christ's statements, and He will test whether the expositions are of God or not. Jesus Christ's teaching is involved in such a manner that only the Holy Spirit can extricate its meaning for us. "He shall lead you into all truth." The Holy Spirit never witnesses to a clever interpretation; the exposition the Holy Spirit will witness to is always amazingly and profoundly simple.

MARCH 11

The Divine Direction

> Early in the morning Abraham got up and saddled his donkey. He took with him two of his servants and his son Isaac. When he had cut enough wood for the burnt offering, he set out for the place God had told him about *(Genesis 22:3)*.

God never fits His word to suit me; He fits me to suit His word. The discernment of God's call does not come in every moment of life but only in rare moments, the moments Our Lord spoke of as "the light" (John 12:35–36); we have to remain true to what we see in those moments; if we do not, we will put back God's purpose in our life. The undercurrent of regret in obeying the call of God arises from conferring with those who do not see with the one called, and if we listen to them we get into darkness. The life of Abraham is an illustration of two things: of unreserved surrender to God, and of God's complete possession of a child of His for His own highest ends.

The Duty of Diligence

Early the next morning Abraham got up and saddled his donkey. He took with him two of his servants and his son Isaac. When he had cut enough wood for the burnt offering, he set out for the place God had told him about" *(Genesis 22:3)*.

A nd Abraham rose up early in the morning."
This phrase is characteristic not only of men and women in the Bible but of God Himself. The revelation of God in the Old Testament is that of a working God. No other religion presents God either as diligent or as suffering, but as an all-in-all principle, ruling in lofty disdain. The God Who reveals Himself to Abraham is One ever intent on the fulfillment of His great designs; and like God, like people. If God is diligent, surely we ought to be diligent in doing our duty to Him. Think how patient and how diligent God has been with us! Over and over again God gets us near the point, and then by some petty individual sulk we spoil it all, and He patiently begins all over again. Think of the vision, "whiter than snow shine," God gave of what He wanted us to be—where has it gone? Has God had to begin all over again from where I left off last time, or have I said—I shall be true to God at all costs, no matter what the isolation?

Sacramental Discipleship

May I never boast except in the cross of our Lord Jesus Christ, through which the world has been crucified to me, and I to the world *(Galatians 6:14)*.

B y the Cross of Christ I am saved from sin; by the Cross I am sanctified; but I never am a sacramental disciple until I deliberately lay myself on the altar of the Cross and give myself over emphatically and entirely to be actually what I am potentially in the sight of God, viz., a member of the Body of Christ. When I swing clear of myself and my own consciousness and give myself over to Jesus Christ, He can use me as a sacrament to nourish other lives.

MARCH 14 _____

Decrease and Increase

"He must become greater; I must become less" *(John 3:30).*

E xamine yourself in the light of these words. It is never that I drag God down into my sympathies; He lifts me clean into His. The more spiritually real I become, the less am I of any account. I become more and more of the nature of a grain of wheat falling into the earth and dying in order that it may bring forth fruit. "He must increase, but I must decrease." I only decrease as He increases, and He only increases in me as I nourish His life by that which decreases me. Am I willing to feed the life of the Son of God in me?

MARCH 15 _____

God's Will Overcoming in Us

You, dear children, are from God and have overcome them, because the one who is in you is greater than the one who is in the world *(1 John 4:4).*

There is no such thing as fate; a human being always has the power to do the incalculable thing. There are fatal issues, but not fate. When God's decrees come to pass it is because men will not turn. God's will is supreme, but God never fights against us; it is self-will that fights against God. When the Spirit of God is at work in him a man lets God's will overcome. There is no fight; it is a higher power easily overcoming.

MARCH 16 _____

Is God Love?

Whoever does not love does not know God, because God is love *(1 John 4:8).*

The love of God cannot make room for sin or self-interest; therefore, the appeal of the love of God is not that of kindness and gentleness, but of holiness. If you take the natural view of the love of God you will become atheistic. If God were love according to our natural view of love He ought never to cause us pain; He ought to allow us to be peaceful; but the first thing God does is to cause us pain and to rouse us wide awake. That is why God looks cruel judged from the human sentimental standpoint; He loves us so much that He will not prevent us being hurt.

MARCH 17 _____

Sacramental Responsibility

Now I rejoice in what was suffered for you, and I fill up in my flesh what is still lacking in regard to Christ's

61

afflictions, for the sake of his body, which is the church *(Colossians 1:24)*.

B y "sacramental responsibility" understand the solemn determination to keep myself notably my Lord's, and to treat as a subtle temptation of the devil the call to take on any responsibility that conflicts with my determined identification with His interests. God's one great interest in men is that they are redeemed; am I identifying myself with that interest?

MARCH 18 _____

The Final Trust

"Though he slay me, yet will I hope in him; I will surely defend my ways to his face" *(Job 13:15)*.

B eware of everything that makes you pose religiously. A conscious pose springs from acquirements, not from vital life.

Experiences of what God has done for me are only stepping-stones; the one great note is—I trust in the Lord Jesus. God's providence can do with me what He likes, make the heavens like brass, earth like hell, my body loathsome—as Job's was; but the soul that is trusting in Jesus gets where Job got—"Though He slay me, yet will I trust in Him"—"I have no idea what God's purpose is, but I rest confidently in Him."

The Hidden Life

"And why do you worry about clothes? See how the lilies of the field grow. They do not labor or spin" *(Matthew 6:28)*.

C onsider the lilies of the field, how they grow"—in the dark! We are apt to consider a lily when it is in the sunshine only, but for the greater part of the year it is buried in the ground. We imagine we are to be always above ground, shedding perfume and looking beautiful; or being continually cut and put into God's showroom to be admired, forgetting altogether that we cannot grow and be cut at the same time. We cannot be as lilies unless we have spent time in the dark, totally ignored. Jesus says, as a disciple, consider your hidden life with God. When we breathe fresh air we are not consciously, exhilaratingly different all the time; but if we continue to take in fresh air, it makes a profound difference. This is true of our life in Christ.

Spiritual Curiosity

Now to you who believe, this stone is precious. But to those who do not believe, "The stone the builders rejected has become the capstone" *(1 Peter 2:7)*.

I n natural life we grow by means of curiosity, and spiritually we grow by the same power. The Spirit of God uses the natural reaction of curiosity to enable us to know more about the One Who is precious. The instinct is not denied, but lifted on to a different platform and turned towards knowing Jesus Christ. As saints our curiosity must not be all abroad; Jesus Christ is the One Who rivets our attention; we become insatiably curious about Him. Think of the avidity with which you devour anything that has to do with expounding the Lord Jesus Christ. "Unto you therefore which believe He is precious."

His Cross and Ours

"And anyone who does not carry his cross and follow me cannot be my disciple" *(Luke 14:27)*.

T he Cross of Christ stands unique and alone; we are never called upon to carry His Cross. Our cross is something that comes only with the peculiar relationship of a disciple to Jesus Christ; it is the evidence that we have denied the right to ourselves. The Cross of Jesus Christ is a revelation; our cross is an experience. Our Lord was not talking about suffering for conscience sake or conviction's sake; men suffer for conscience sake who know nothing about Jesus Christ and owe Him no allegiance; men suffer for conviction's sake if they are worth their salt, whether they are Christians or not.

What the Cross was to our Lord, such also in measure was it to be to those who followed Him. The Cross is the pain involved in doing the will of God.

Bane and Blessing in the Cross

"All men will hate you because of me, but he who stands firm to the end will be saved. . . . A student is not above his teacher, nor a servant above his master. It is enough for the student to be like his teacher, and the servant like his master. If the head of the house has been called Beelzebub, how much more the members of his household!" *(Matthew 10:22, 24–25).*

T hese verses need to be re-read because we are apt to think that Jesus Christ took all the bitterness, and we get all the blessing. It is true that we get the blessing, but we must never forget that the wine of life is made out of crushed grapes; to follow Him will involve bruising in the lives of the disciples as the purpose of God did in His own life. The thing that makes us whimper is that we will look for justice. If in your Christian work you look for justice you will soon put yourself in a bandage and give way to self-pity and discouragement. Never look for justice, but never cease to give it; and never allow anything you meet with to sour your relationship to men through Jesus Christ. "Love as I have loved you."

Preaching the Cross With Passion

But we preach Christ crucified: a stumbling block to Jews and foolishness to Gentiles *(1 Corinthians 1:23).*

N ever confuse the Cross of Christ with the benefits that flow from it. For all his doctrine, Paul's one great passion was the Cross of Christ, not salvation, nor sanctification, but the great truth that God so loved the world that He gave His only begotten Son. Consequently you never find Paul artificial, or making a feeble statement. Every doctrine he taught had the blood and the power of God in it. There is an amazing force of spirit in all he said because the great passion behind it was not that he wanted men to be holy, that was secondary, but that he had come to understand what God meant by the Cross of Christ. If I have the idea of personal holiness only, of being put in God's showroom, I will never come anywhere near seeing what God wants; but when once I have come where Paul is, and God is enabling me to understand what the Cross of Christ means, then nothing can ever turn me.

MARCH 24 _____

Preaching the Crucified With Passion

For I resolved to know nothing while I was with you except Jesus Christ and him crucified (1 Corinthians 2:2).

Y ou cannot be profoundly moved by a sentiment or by an idea of holiness, but you can be moved by a passion; and the old writers used to speak of the Cross as the Passion of Our Lord. The one impression left by Paul, whether his words were stinging or comforting, for praise or for condemnation, was Christ and Him crucified, not risen and exalted, but *crucified*. The reason some of us have no power, no sense of awe, in our preaching, is that we have no passion for God, only a passion for Humanity. The one thing we have to do is to exhibit Jesus Christ crucified, to lift

Him up all the time and "I, if I be lifted up, will draw all men unto Me." Paul had one passion only; he had seen the light of the knowledge of the glory of God in the face of Jesus Christ. Who is Jesus Christ? God exalted in Christ crucified.

MARCH 25

The Cross, a Stumbling Block

But we preach Christ crucified: a stumbling block to Jews and foolishness to Gentiles *(1 Corinthians 1:23)*.

There is no such thing as *sin* to intellectual reasoning, and consequently no meaning in the Cross, because that point of view rules out what the Bible bases everything on. The Bible bases everything on the hiatus produced by sin between God and man, as well as on the Cross where Jesus Christ deals with sin. When intellectual reasoning comes to the Cross it is embarrassed because it looks on the Cross as the death of a martyr, one who lived beyond his dispensation. According to the New Testament the Cross is not the death of a man; it is the Cross of God.

MARCH 26

The Grape and the Wine

"This is to my Father's glory, that you bear much fruit, showing yourselves to be my disciples" *(John 15:8)*.

If you want to remain a full-orbed grape you must keep out of God's hands for He will crush you; wine cannot be had in any other way. The curse in Christian work is that we want to preserve ourselves in God's museum; what God wants is to see where Jesus Christ's men and women are. The saints are always amongst the unofficial crowd, the crowd that is not noticed, and their one dominant note is Jesus Christ.

MARCH 27 _____

God's Heart Revealed

About the ninth hour Jesus cried out in a loud voice, *"Eloi, Eloi, lama sabachthani?"* —which means, *"My God, my God, why have you forsaken me?" (Matthew 27:46).*

T he Cross is the crystallized point in history where Eternity merges with Time. The cry on the Cross, "My God, My God, why hast Thou forsaken Me" is not the desolation of an isolated individual: It is the revelation of the heart of God face to face with the sin of man, and going deeper down than man's sin can ever go in inconceivable heartbreak in order that every sin-stained, hell-deserving sinner might be absolutely redeemed.

MARCH 28 _____

Propitiation Through the Cross

He is the atoning sacrifice for our sins, and not only for ours but also for the sins of the whole world *(1 John 2:2).*

I f the significance of Christ as the propitiation is immense, the domain to which His propitiation applies is limitless also. Sinfulness against Christ is as

limitless as the propitiation. . . . We are not to talk sentimental nonsense about the Universal Fatherhood of God;
to knock the bottom board out of Redemption by saying
that God is love and of course He will forgive sin. . . . The
only ground on which God can forgive sin and reinstate us
in His favour, is through the Cross of Christ, and in no other
way.

MARCH 29 _____

The Cleansing Blood

But if we walk in the light, as he is in the light, we have
fellowship with one another, and the blood of Jesus, his
Son, purifies us from all sin *(1 John 1:7)*.

When we speak of the blood of Jesus Christ cleansing
us from all sin, we do not mean the physical blood
shed on Calvary, but the whole life of the Son of God
which was poured out to redeem the world. All the
perfections of the essential nature of God were in that
blood, and all the holiest attainments of mankind as well. It
was the life of the perfection of Deity that was poured out
on Calvary.

MARCH 30 _____

The Wonder of Redemption

The next day John saw Jesus coming toward him and
said, "Look, the Lamb of God, who takes away the sin
of the world!" *(John 1:29)*.

G od Almighty took the problem of the sin of the world on His own shoulders, and it made Him stoop; He rehabilitated the whole human race, that is, He put the human race back where He designed it to be, and any one of us in our actual conditions can enter into union with God on the ground of Jesus Christ's Redemption. . . . A man cannot redeem himself; Redemption is absolutely finished and complete; its reference to individual men is a question of their individual action.

MARCH 31 _____

Thinking God's Thoughts

"For my thoughts are not your thoughts, neither are your ways my ways," declares the LORD *(Isaiah 55:8).*

A s soon as we begin to examine the foundations of our salvation we are up against the thoughts of God, and as Christians we ought to be busy thinking God's thoughts after Him. That is where we fall short to-day, we are delighted with the fact that "Once I was this, and now I am that," but simply to have a vivid experience is not sufficient if we are to be at our best for God. It is because Christians have refused to think on Christian lines that Satan has come in as an angel of light and switched off numbers of God's children in their heads, with the result that there is a divorce between heart and head.

God in the Commonplace

The Lord said, "Go out and stand on the mountain in the presence of the Lord, for the Lord is about to pass by." Then a great and powerful wind tore the mountains apart and shattered the rocks before the Lord, but the Lord was not in the wind. After the wind there was an earthquake, but the Lord was not in the earthquake. After the earthquake came a fire, but the Lord was not in the fire. And after the fire came a gentle whisper *(1 Kings 19:11–12).*

T he ministrations of God come over and over again in the most commonplace manner possible. We look for some great big alteration, something marvellous like the wind, or an earthquake, or fire; and the voice of God tells us to do what the most ordinary voice we know might tell us to do. "And after the fire a still small voice"—i.e., "a sound of gentle stillness"—the one thing the Lord was in.

The Revealing Crisis

Jesus replied, "No one who puts his hand to the plow and looks back is fit for service in the kingdom of God" *(Luke 9:62).*

O ver and over again men and women who should stand in the forefront for God are knocked clean out when a crisis comes; the reason is not external wrongdoing, but there is something in which Jesus Christ has not had His right of way, something has never been given up, and their discipleship is marred. God gives us ample opportunity of proving whether we have really given up the right to ourselves to Jesus Christ. The one who has offers no hindrance to the Holy Spirit working through him.

Baffled!

"Why is light given to those in misery, and life to the bitter of soul, to those who long for death that does not come, who search for it more than for hidden treasure, who are filled with gladness and rejoice when they reach the grave? Why is life given to a man whose way is hidden, whom God has hedged in? For sighing comes to me instead of food; my groans pour out like water. What I feared has come upon me; what I dreaded has happened to me. I have no peace, no quietness; I have no rest, but only turmoil" *(Job 3:20–26).*

T he experience of being baffled is common to us all, and the more religious and thoughtful a man is, the more intensely is he baffled. With regard to your own baffling, recognize it and state it, but don't state it dishonestly to yourself. Don't say you are not baffled if you are, and don't tell a lie in order to justify your belief in God. If you are in the dark, don't take refuge in any subterfuge which you know is not true. Never take an answer that satisfies your mind only; insist on an answer that satisfies more than your mind.

_____

Wind, Earthquake and Fire

The Lord said, "Go out and stand on the mountain in
the presence of the LORD, for the LORD is about to pass
by." Then a great and powerful wind tore the mountains
apart and shattered the rocks before the LORD, but the
Lord SC was not in the wind. After the wind there was
an earthquake, but the LORD was not in the earthquake.
After the earthquake came a fire, but the LORD was not in
the fire. And after the fire came a gentle whisper
(1 Kings 19: 11–12).

T oday there are colossal forces abroad and God is
   using them as His instruments, but He is not "in"
them; that is, they are not God. It is a misconception to
imagine that God is bound up in His instruments; He uses
forces and powers for His own ends, but they must never
be mistaken for Himself. An instrument conveys God's
message, and a man used by God ought to be a holy man:
but it does not always follow that he is (cf. Matt. 7:21–22).

_____

"In Adam" or "In Christ"

For as in Adam all die, so in Christ all will be made alive
(1 Corinthians 15:22).

T he terms "in Adam," "in Christ," are not mystical
   terms, but actual revelations of man's condition.
When we are "in Adam" we get down to the desolating
desert aspect of life. Take love—the most abiding thing
about love is its tragedy; or life, the most desolating thing

about life is its climax, death. When we are "in Christ" the whole thing is reversed. We read that "Jesus advanced in wisdom and stature and in favour with God and man"— He never ate of the fruit of the tree of good and evil; He knew evil only by contrast with good. When a man is born from above, the desolating desert aspect of life goes. There is no sadness now in natural love; it ends nowhere but in the heart of God; "in Christ" life knows no death, it goes on more and more fully. If you want to know God's original design for man, you see it in Jesus Christ; He was easily Master of the life on the earth, in the air, and in the sea, not as God but as Man; it was the human in Jesus that was master.

APRIL 6 _____

The Door of Destitution

"Blessed are the poor in spirit, for theirs is the kingdom of heaven" *(Matthew 5:3)*.

Our Lord begins where we would never begin, at the point of human destitution. The greatest blessing a man ever gets from God is the realization that if he is going to enter into His Kingdom it must be through the door of destitution. Naturally we do not want to begin there; that is why the appeal of Jesus is of no use until we come face to face with realities; then the only One worth listening to is the Lord. We learn to welcome the patience of Jesus only when we get to the point of human destitution. It is not that God *will* not do anything for us until we get there, but that He *cannot*. God can do nothing for me if I am sufficient for myself. When we come to the place of destitution spiritually we find the Lord waiting, and saying, "If any man thirst, let him come unto Me, and drink."

The Bank of Faith

Then Jesus told him, "Because you have seen me, you have believed; blessed are those who have not seen and yet have believed" *(John 20:29).*

S eeing is never believing: we interpret what we see in the light of what we believe. Faith is confidence in God before you see God emerging; therefore the nature of faith is that it must be tried. To say "Oh yes, I believe God will triumph" may be so much credence smeared over with religious phraseology; but when you are up against things it is quite another matter to say, "I believe God will win through." The trial of our faith gives us a good banking account in the heavenly places, and when the next trial comes our wealth there will tide us over. If we have confidence in God beyond the actual earthly horizons, we shall see the lie at the heart of the fear, and our faith will win through in every detail. Jesus said that men ought always to pray and not "cave in"—"Don't look at the immediate horizon and don't take the facts you see and say they are the reality; they are actuality; the Reality lies behind with God."

"Having Done All to Stand"

Put on the full armor of God so that you can take your stand against the devil's schemes. For our struggle is not against flesh and blood, but against the rulers, against the authorities, against the powers of this dark world and against the spiritual forces of evil in the heavenly realms. Therefore put on the full armor of God, so that when the day of evil comes, you may be able to stand your ground, and after you have done everything, to stand. Stand firm then, with the belt of of truth buckled around your waist, with the breastplate of righteousness in place, and with your feet fitted with the readiness that comes from the gospel of peace. In addition to all this, take up the shield of faith, with which you can extinguish all the flaming arrows of the evil one. Take the helmet of salvation and the sword of the Spirit, which is the word of God. And pray in the Spirit on all occasions with all kinds of prayers and requests. With this in mind, be alert and always keep on praying for all the saints. Pray also for me, that whenever I open my mouth, words may be given me so that I will fearlessly make known the mystery of the gospel, for which I am an ambassador in chains. Pray that I may declare it fearlessly, as I should (*Ephesians 6:11–20*).

P aul is writing from prison; he knows all about the Roman soldier whose armour he is describing, for he was chained to one of them. "I am an ambassador in a chain," he says.

These verses are not a picture of how to fight, but of how not to fight. If you have not put on the armour, you will have to fight; but "having put on the whole armour of God," says Paul, "then *stand.*" There are times when

God's servants are sent out to attack, to storm the citadel, but the counsel given here is as to how we are to hold the position which has been gained. We need to learn this conservation of energy, "having done all, to stand," manifesting the full power of God.

APRIL 9 _____

Hard Words

The disciples were even more amazed, and said to each other, "Who then can be saved?" (Mark 10:26).

J esus Christ says a great deal that we listen to, but we do not hear it. When we *do* hear, His words are amazingly hard. These words were so hard that His very disciples were staggered—"And they that heard it said, 'Who then can be saved?' " Jesus did not seem the least solicitous that the rich young ruler should do what He told him; He made no attempt to keep him with Him; He simply said—"Sell all that thou hast, . . . and come, follow me."

APRIL 10 _____

Deliberate Detachment

Jesus answered, "If you want to be perfect, go, sell your possessions and give to the poor, and you will have treasure in heaven. Then come, follow me" (Matthew 19:21).

S ell all that thou hast and distribute unto the poor." There is a general principle here and a particular reference. We are always in danger of taking the particular reference for the general principle and evading the general principle. The particular reference here is to selling material goods. The rich young ruler had deliberately to be destitute, deliberately to distribute, deliberately to discern where his treasure was, and to devote himself to Jesus Christ. The principle underlying it is that I must detach myself from everything I possess.

APRIL 11

Spiritual Concentration

So I turned to the Lord God and pleaded with him in prayer and petition, in fasting, and in sackcloth and ashes (Daniel 9:3).

A nd I set my face . . ."
We discern spiritual truth not by intellectual curiosity or research, but by entreating the favour of the Lord, that is, by prayer and by no other way, not even by obedience, because obedience is apt to have an idea of merit. If we are not concentrated we affect a great many attitudes; but when we "set our faces unto the Lord God" all affectation is gone—the religious pose, the devout pose, the pious pose, all go instantly when we determine to concentrate; our attention is so concentrated that we have no time to wonder how we look. "This one thing I do . . ." says Paul; his whole attention was fixed on God. Is my mind fixed entirely on God, or on service for God?

The Spirit Here to Be Received

"If you then, though you are evil, know how to give good gifts to your children, how much more will your Father in heaven give the Holy Spirit to those who ask him!" *(Luke 11:13).*

We are told by some that it is foolish to ask God for the Holy Spirit because this is the dispensation of the Holy Spirit. Thank God it is! God's mighty Spirit is with all men; He impinges on men's lives at all points and in unexpected places; but the great need is to receive the Holy Spirit that He may do *in* us all that Jesus Christ did *for* us on the Cross. There stands the mighty charter for every man and woman who will put it to the test— "If ye then, being evil, know how to give good gifts unto your children: how much more shall your Heavenly Father give the Holy Spirit to them that ask him?" (Luke 11:13).

The regenerating and sanctifying work of the Holy Spirit is to incorporate us into Christ until we are living witnesses to Him.

Submitting to His Word and Will

So Jesus said, "When you have lifted up the Son of Man, then you will know who I am and that I do nothing on my own but speak just what the Father has taught me" *(John 8:28).*

The secret of Our Lord's holy speech was that He habitually submitted His intelligence to His Father.

Whenever problems pressed on the human side, as they did in the temptation, Our Lord had within Himself the Divine remembrance that every problem had been solved in counsel with His Father before He became Incarnate (cf. Rev. 13:8), and that therefore the one thing for Him was to do the will of His Father, and to do it His Father's way. Satan tried to hasten Him, tried to make Him face the problems as a Man and do God's will in His own way: "The Son can do nothing of himself, but what he seeth the Father doing."

Are we intellectually insubordinate, spiritually stiff-necked, dictating to God in pious phraseology what we intend to let Him make us, hunting through the Bible to back up our pet theories? Or have we learned the secret of submitting our intelligence and our reasoning to Jesus Christ's word and will as He submitted His mind to His Father?

APRIL 14 _____

"In the Form of a Servant"

But made himself nothing, taking the very nature of a servant, being made in human likeness *(Philippians 2:7)*.

Our Lord took upon Him habitually the part of a slave: "I am among you as he that serveth." Consequently He could be "put upon" to any extent, unless His Father prevented it (cf. John 19:11) or His Father's honour was at stake (cf. Mark 11:15–19). It was our Lord's right to be "in the form of God," but He renounced that right and took "the form of a bond-servant," not the form of a nobleman

but of a slave. Our Lord crowned the words that the powers
of this world detest—*servant, obedience, humility, service.*

APRIL 15 _____

The Divine Self-emptying

But made himself nothing, taking the very nature of a
servant, being made in human likeness *(Philippians 2:7).*

J esus Christ effaced the Godhead in Himself so
effectually that men without the Spirit of God
despised Him. No one without the Spirit of God, or apart
from a sudden revelation from God, ever saw the true self
of Jesus whilst He was on earth. He was "as a root out of a
dry ground," thoroughly disadvantaged in the eyes of
everyone not convicted of sin. The reference in 2 Corinthians 8:9 is not to a wealthy *man* becoming poor, but to a
wealthy *God* becoming poor for men. The purpose of the
Incarnation was to remove sin from human nature. To
those who seek after wisdom the preaching of Christ
crucified is foolishness; but when a man knows that his life
is twisted, that the mainspring is wrong, he is in the state of
heart and mind to understand why it was necessary for God
to become Incarnate. The doctrine of the Self-limitation of
Jesus is clear to our hearts first, not to our heads. We
cannot form the mind of Christ unless we have His Spirit,
nor can we understand Our Lord's teaching apart from His
Spirit. We cannot see through it; but when once we receive
His Spirit we know implicitly what He means.

"Obedient Unto Death"

> And being found in appearance as a man, he humbled himself and became obedient to death—even death on a cross! *(Philippians 2:8).*

R ight at the threshold of His manhood Our Lord took upon Him His vocation, which was to bear away the sin of the world—by *identification,* not by sympathy (John 1:29). Our Lord's object in becoming Deity Incarnate was to redeem mankind, and Satan's final onslaught in the Garden of Gethsemane was against Our Lord *as Son of Man,* viz., that the purpose of His Incarnation would fail. The profundity of His agony has to do with the fulfilling of His destiny. The Cross is a triumph for *the Son of Man;* any and every man has freedom of access straight to the throne of God by right of what Our Lord accomplished through His death on the Cross.

Habit Forming . . . Character Building

> For this very reason, make every effort to add to your faith goodness; and to goodness, knowledge; and to knowledge, self-control; and to self-control, perseverance; and to perseverance, godliness; and to godliness, brotherly kindness; and to brotherly kindness, love *(2 Peter 1:5–7).*

A lways distinguish between the defects of a growing life and the vices of a mature life. Be as merciless as God can make you with the vices of a mature life, but be endlessly patient with the defects of a growing life. A young life is always in chaos, but there is one main trend coming out all the time, and that trend can be garrisoned by intercessory prayer.

God never makes character; God puts into us the disposition of His Son, and on that basis we have to form character. As we form the habit of doing things in accordance with the disposition of Jesus Christ we are backed by inward supplies of God's grace. Every habit begins with difficulty. Habit is a mechanical process of which we have ceased to become conscious. A man who is right with God does the right thing instinctively. "Add to your faith virtue. . . ." These things do not emerge until we so form the habit of doing them that they become characteristic of our lives.

APRIL 18 _____

His Love Gift to God, and Ours

"For them I sanctify myself, that they too may be truly sanctified" *(John 17:19)*.

I f we have entered into the experience of sanctification, what are we doing with our holy selves? Do we every morning we waken thank God that we have a self to give to Him, a self that He has purified and adjusted and baptized with the Holy Ghost so that we might sacrifice it to Him? Sacrifice in its essence is the exuberant, passionate love-gift of the best I have to the one I love best. The best gift the Son of God had was His holy Manhood, and He gave that as a love-gift to God that He might use it as an Atonement for the world. "He poured out his soul unto death," and that is to be the characteristic of our lives. God is at perfect liberty to waste us if he chooses. We are sanctified for one purpose only, that we might sanctify our sanctification and give it to God.

Circumstances, Dark and Bright

> And we know that in all things God works for the good of those who love him, who have been called according to his purpose *(Romans 8:28).*

N ever confound circumstances with environment. Environment is the element in our circumstances that fits our disposition. We cannot control our circumstances, but we are the deciders of our own environment. We have to remember the "altogetherness" of circumstances (cf. Romans 8:28). If your circumstances are dark blue just now, remember the time when they were bright pink. It is not the dark blue circumstances or the bright pink circumstances that work for good, but the "togetherness" of them that works for good. Circumstances either produce energy and smeddum (i.e., grit, courage and pluck) or enervation. The marvelous thing about the life of God in us is that there is no reaction of exhaustion, but a continual pouring in all the time (Psalm 87:7). If we work from the real source of energy, viz., our relationship to God; everything that happens brings more life and fuller, with no reaction.

Enjoying the Disagreeable

I know what it is to be in need, and I know what it is to have plenty. I have learned the secret of being content in any and every situation, whether well fed or hungry, whether living in plenty or in want. I can do everything through him who gives me strength *(Philippians 4:12– 13).*

It is one thing to go into the disagreeable by God's engineering, but another thing to go into it by choice. If God puts us there He is amply sufficient. No matter how difficult the circumstances may be, if we will let Jesus Christ manifest Himself in them, it will prove to be a new means of exhibiting the wonderful perfection and extraordinary purity of the Son of God. This keen enthusiasm of letting the Son of God manifest Himself in us is the only thing that will keep us enjoying the disagreeable.

The Joy and Peace of the Satisfied

Made us alive with Christ even when we were dead in transgressions—it is by grace you have been saved. And God raised us up with Christ and seated us with him in the heavenly realms in Christ Jesus *(Ephesians 2: 5–6).*

If all Jesus Christ came to do was to upset me, make me unfit for my work, upset my friendships and my life, produce disturbance and misery and distress, then I wish He had never come. But that is not all He came to do. He came to lift us up into the heavenly places where He is

Himself. The whole claim of the Redemption of Jesus Christ is that He can satisfy the last aching abyss of the human soul, not hereafter only, but here and now. Satisfaction does not mean stagnation; it means the knowledge that we have the right type of life for our souls. The phrase in the hymn, "Oh the peace my Saviour gives," is a Biblical one. That peace is the deepest thing a human personality can know, it is almighty. The apostle Paul emphasized the hilarity of life. "Be not drunk with wine, . . . but be filled with the Spirit." Enthusiasm is the idea, intoxicated with the life of God. Psalm 73 is a description of the bad man having all that heart can desire; that is satisfaction without God. A bad man has a hilarious time, and a man whose life is right has a hilarious time. The healthy pagan and the healthy saint are the ones described in God's Book as hilarious; all in between are diseased and more or less sick. MK

The Worldling and the Christian

And I'll say to myself, "You have plenty of good things laid up for many years. Take life easy; eat, drink, and be merry" *(Luke 12:19)*.

N ever have the idea that a worldling is unhappy—a worldling is perfectly happy, as thoroughly happy as a Christian. The persons who are unhappy are the worldlings or the Christians if they are not at one with the principle that binds them. When a worldling is not a worldling at heart, he is miserable; and when a Christian is not a Christian at heart, he is miserable; he carries his religion like a headache instead of something that is worth having. A worldling is one who has wisely kept within bounds of the disposition

which the Bible alone reveals as the disposition of sin, viz.,
my claim to my right to myself. When once that is broken
into by overt acts of wrongdoing, the worldling is miserable,
and he ceases to be a true worldling. Remember, then, the
two things that disintegrate the devil's kingdom—breaking
out into acts of sin and the conviction of the Spirit of God.
This is the solution of a number of moral problems.

Here for One Thing Only

So we make it our goal to please him, whether we are at
home in the body or away from it *(2 Corinthians 5:9).*

I am here for one thing only, for Jesus Christ to
manifest Himself in me." That is to be the steadfast
habit of a Christian's life. Whenever we think we are of use
to God, we hinder Him. We have to form the habit of
letting God carry on His work through us without let or
hindrance as He did through Jesus, and He will use us in
ways He dare not let us see. We have to efface every other
thought but that of Jesus Christ; it is not done once for all;
we have to be always doing it. If once you have seen that
Jesus Christ is all in all, make the habit of letting Him be all
in all. It will mean that you not only have implicit faith that
He is all in all, but that you go through the trial of your faith
and prove that He is. After sanctification God delights to put
us into places where He can make us wealthy.

The Witness of the Spirit-filled Life

When they saw the courage of Peter and John and realized that they were unschooled, ordinary men, they were astonished and they took note that these men had been with Jesus *(Acts 4:13)*.

W e have the Bible bound in morocco, bound in all kinds of beautiful leather. What we need is the Bible bound in shoe leather." That is exactly the teaching of Our Lord. After the disciples had received the Holy Spirit, they became witnesses to Jesus; their lives spoke more eloquently than their lips—" and they took knowledge of them, that they had been with Jesus." The Holy Spirit being imparted to us and expressed through us is the manifested exhibition that God can do all that His Book states He can. It is those who have received the Holy Spirit who understand the will of God and "grow up into Him in all things." When the Scriptures are made quick and powerful by the Holy Spirit, they fit every need of life.

The Peril of Impulse

"But when he, the Spirit of truth, comes, he will guide you into all truth. He will not speak on his own; he will speak only what he hears, and he will tell you what is yet to come. He will bring glory to me by taking from what is mine and making it known to you" *(John 16:13–14)*.

A ny impulse which does not lead to the glorification of Jesus Christ has the snare of Satan behind it. People say, "How am I to know whether my impulse is from the Holy Spirit or from my own imagination?" Very easily. Jesus Christ gave us the simplest, most easy-to-be-understood tests for guidance—"The Holy Ghost . . . shall teach you all things, and shall bring all things to your remembrance, whatsoever I have said unto you"; the Holy Spirit "will guide you into all truth: for He shall not speak of Himself." Beware of any religious experience which glorifies you and not Jesus Christ.

APRIL 26 _____

The Crown and the Cross

As he was praying, the appearance of his face changed, and his clothes became as bright as a flash of lightning *(Luke 9:29)*.

But we see Jesus, who was made a little lower than the angels, now crowned with glory and honor because he suffered death, so that by the grace of God he might taste death for everyone (Hebrews 2:9).

We say, "No cross, no crown"; in the life of Our Lord the crown of the glory of the Transfiguration came before the Cross. You never know Jesus Christ, and Him crucified, unless you have seen Him transfigured in all His transcendent majesty and glory; the Cross to you is nothing but the cross of a martyr. If you have seen Jesus glorified, you know that the Cross is the revelation of God's judgment of sin, that on the Cross Our Lord bore the whole massed sin of the human race. "Him Who knew no sin He made to be sin on our behalf." No wonder we say:

Since mine eyes have looked on Jesus
I've lost sight of all beside.

Have we seen Him, "crowned with glory and honour"?

APRIL 27 _____

Be Spiritually Tenacious

Since you have kept my command to endure patiently, I
will also keep you from the hour of trial that is going to
come upon the whole world to test those who live on the
earth *(Revelation 3:10)*.

One of the greatest strains in life is the strain of waiting
for God. "Because thou didst keep the word of My
patience." God takes the saints like a bow which he
stretches and at a certain point the saint says, "I can't stand
any more," but God does not heed; He goes on stretching
because He is aiming at His mark, not ours, and the
patience of the saints is that they "hang in" until God lets
the arrow fly.

If your hopes are being disappointed just now it means
that they are being purified. There is nothing noble the
human mind has ever hoped for or dreamed of that will not
be fulfilled. Don't jump to conclusions too quickly; one or
two things lie unsolved, and the biggest test of all is that
God looks as if He were totally indifferent.

APRIL 28 _____

Partakers of His Holiness

Our fathers disciplined us for a little while as they thought
best; but God disciplines us for our good, that we may
share in his holiness *(Hebrews 12:10)*.

T he characteristic of the holiness of Almighty God is that it is absolute; it is impossible to antagonize or strain it. The characteristic of the holiness of Jesus is that it manifested itself by means of antagonism; it was a holiness that could be tested (see Hebrews 4:15). The Son of God, as Son of Man, transformed innocence into holy character bit by bit as things opposed; He did not exhibit an immutable holiness but a holiness of which we can be made partakers—"that we might be partakers of His holiness" (Hebrews 12:10). Jesus Christ revealed what a normal man should be and in so doing showed how we may become all that God wants us to be.

APRIL 29 _____

Do Not Panic

"You will hear of wars and rumors of wars, but see to it that you are not alarmed. Such things must happen, but the end is still to come" *(Matthew 24:6)*.

T hat is either the statement of a madman or of a Being who has power to put something into a man and keep him free from panic, even in the midst of the awful terror of war. The basis of panic is always cowardice. Our Lord teaches us to look things full in the face. He says— "When you hear of wars, don't be scared." It is the most natural thing in the world to be scared, and the clearest evidence that God's grace is at work in our hearts is when we do not get into panics. Our Lord insists on the inevitableness of peril. He says, "You must lay your account with war, with hatred, and with death."

God's Hidden Purpose

Immediately Jesus made his disciples get into the boat and go on ahead of him to Bethsaida, while he dismissed the crowd. After leaving them, he went into the hills to pray. When evening came, the boat was in the middle of the lake, and he was alone on land. He saw the disciples straining at the oars, because the wind was against them. About the fourth watch of the night he went out to them, walking on the lake. He was about to pass by them, but when they saw him walking on the lake, they thought he was a ghost. They cried out, because they all saw him and were terrified. Immediately he spoke to them and said, "Take courage! It is I. Don't be afraid." Then he climbed into the boat with them, and the wind died down. They were completely amazed, for they had not understood about the loaves; their hearts were hardened *(Mark 6:45–52).*

T here was no point of rest for the natural minds of the disciples as to what Jesus was after—it was the deep, the dark, and the dreadful. Our Lord's purpose was that they should see Him walking on the sea. We have an idea that God is leading us to a certain goal, a desired haven; He is not. The question of getting to a particular end is a mere incident. "For I know the plans that I am planning for you, saith the Lord, plans of welfare, and not of calamity, to give you end and expectation" (Jeremiah 29:11). What men call the process, God calls the end. If you can stay in the midst of the turmoil unperplexed and calm because you see Jesus, that is God's purpose in your life; not that you may be able to say "I have done this and that and now it's all right." God's purpose for you is that you depend upon Him and His power *now;* that you see Him walking on the waves—no shore in sight, no success, just the absolute certainty that it is all right because you see Him.

"Silent Unto God"

Find rest O my soul, in God alone; my hope comes from him *(Psalm 62:5)*

M y soul, be silent unto God." Rouse your soul out of its drowsiness to consider God. Fix your attention on God, on the great themes of His Redemption and His holiness, on the great and glorious outlines of His character; be silent to Him there; then be as busy as you like in the ordinary affairs of life. Be like the Lord Jesus; when He was sound asleep in the fishing boat He knew that His Father would waken Him when He wanted Him. This is a marvellous picture of confidence in God.

The Blessing of Ownership

And you are of Christ, and Christ is of God *(1 Corinthians 3:23).*

T he Spirit of God brings us into the realization of our ownership, and the instinct of ownership becomes a tremendous wealth in the life. "All things are yours." Paul prays that the eyes of our understanding may be enlightened that we may know what is ours in Christ Jesus.

No personality, from the tiniest child to Almighty God, is

without this sense of ownership. How wonderfully sprightly a dog looks when he is owned! How weary and hangdog we become when we are convicted of sin; but when we experience God's salvation, we straighten up immediately, everything is altered. We can fling our heads back and look the world in the face because the Lord is ours and we are His. A dominant ownership, such as the Lord's, means that we own everything He owns. "The meek shall inherit the earth."

MAY 3 _____

The Deepest Longing

What is more, I consider everything a loss compared to the surpassing greatness of knowing Christ Jesus my Lord, for whose sake I have lost all things. I consider them rubbish, that I may gain Christ and be found in him, not having a righteousness of my own that comes from the law, but that which is through faith in Christ— the righteousness that comes from God and is by faith. I want to know Christ and the power of his resurrection and the fellowship of sharing in his sufferings, becoming like him in his death, and so, somehow, to attain to the resurrection from the dead. Not that I have already obtained all this, or have already been made perfect, but I press on to take hold of that for which Christ Jesus took hold of me" *(Philippians 3:8–12).*

You are getting tired of life as it is, tired of yourself as you are, getting sour with regard to the setting of your life; lift your eyes for one moment to Jesus Christ. Do you want, more than you want your food, more than you want your sleep, more than you want anything under heaven, or in heaven, that Jesus Christ might so identify you with Himself that you are His first and last and for ever? God grant that the great longing desire of your heart may begin to awaken as it has never done; not only the desire for the forgiveness of sin, but the identification with Jesus Himself until you say, "I live, yet not I, but Christ liveth in me."

MAY 4

Faith in the Great Redemption

> When he had received the drink Jesus said, "It is finished." With that, he bowed his head and gave up his spirit *(John 19:30).*

We can never expound the Redemption, but we must have strong unshaken faith in it so that we are not swept off our feet by actual things. That the devil and man are allowed to do as they like is a mere episode in the providence of God. Everything that has been touched by sin and the devil has been redeemed; we are to live in the world immovably banked in that faith. Unless we have faith in the Redemption, all our activities are fussy impertinences which tell God He is doing nothing. We destroy our souls serving Jesus Christ, instead of abiding in Him. Jesus Christ is not working out the Redemption, it is complete; we are working it out, and beginning to realize it by obedience. Our practical life is to be moulded by our belief in the Redemption, and our declared message will be in accordance with our belief. If we say we believe "It is finished," we must not blaspheme God by unbelief in any domain of our practical life.

The Frontiers of Death

Jesus said to them, "I tell you the truth, unless you eat the flesh of the Son of Man and drink his blood, you have no life in you" *(John 6:53)*.

This is not a sad statement, but a joyful one. Whenever we think we can get the life of God by obedience or prayer or some kind of discipline, we are wrong. We must realize the frontiers of death, that there is no more chance of our entering into the life of God than a mineral has of entering the vegetable kingdom; we can only enter into the Kingdom of God if God will stoop down and lift us up. That is exactly what Jesus Christ promises to do. The bedrock of spiritual life as our Lord taught is poverty—"Blessed are the poor in spirit," not, "Blessed are the strong-willed, or the prayerful, or the consecrated," but, "Blessed is the man who knows he is weak." When we get there the surprise of God's life may come at any time.

The Springs of Love

"I have made you known to them, and will continue to make you known in order that the love you have for me may be in them and that I myself may be in them" *(John 17:26)*.

The springs of love are in God; that means love cannot be found anywhere else. It is absurd for us to try and find the love of God in our hearts naturally; it is not there any more than the life of Jesus Christ is there. Love and life are in God and in Jesus Christ and in the Holy Spirit Whom God gives to us, not because we merit Him, but according to His own particular graciousness. We cannot say in the abstract, "I am going to love my enemies," because naturally we hate them; but when we have a real actual enemy if the love of God is in us, we find we do not hate him. The point is that the springs of love are in the Holy Spirit, not in us. We cannot order the Holy Spirit to come into us; we believe in God, He does the rest.

MAY 7 _____

Willing Poverty for God

For you know the grace of our Lord Jesus Christ, that though he was rich, yet for your sakes he became poor, so that you through his poverty might become rich (2 Corinthians 8:9).

To be willingly poor for God is to strip myself of all things for the sake of Jesus Christ. One of the greatest snares is built on what is really a great truth, viz., that every man has Christ in himself. The pernicious use that is made of that statement is that therefore man draws power from himself. Never! Jesus Christ never drew power from Himself: He drew it always from without Himself, viz., from His Father. "The Son can do nothing of Himself" (John 5:19 and 30). Beware of being rich spiritually on earth; only be rich spiritually in heaven. Jesus said to the rich young ruler, "If you will strip yourself and have no riches here, you will lay up for yourself treasure in heaven." Treasure in heaven is faith that has been tried (cf. Revelation 3:18). Immediately we begin to have fellowship with Jesus we

97

have to live the life of faith at all costs; it may be bitter to begin with, but afterwards it is ineffably and indescribably sweet—willing poverty for God, a determined going outside myself and every earthly thing.

The "If" of Discipleship

"If anyone comes to me and does not hate his father and mother, his wife and children, his brothers and sisters— yes, even his own life–he cannot be my disciple. And anyone who does not carry his cross and follow me cannot be my disciple" *(Luke 14:26–27).*

J esus Christ always talked about discipleship with an "If." We are at perfect liberty to toss our spiritual head and say, "No thank you, that is a bit too stern for me," and the Lord will never say a word; we can do exactly what we like; He will never plead, but the opportunity is there, "If . . ."

After all, it is the great stern call of Jesus that fascinates men and women quicker than anything. It is not the gospel of being saved from hell and enjoying heaven that attracts men, saving in a very shallow mood; it is Christ crucified that attracts men; Jesus said so—"I, if I be lifted up from the earth, will draw all men unto Me." Jesus Christ never attracts us by the unspeakable bliss of Paradise; He attracts us by an ugly beam.

Confession of the Childlike Attitude

I know, O LORD, that a man's life is not his own; it is not
for man to direct his steps *(Jeremiah 10:23)*.

L ord, I know that the way of man is not in himself: it is
not in man that walketh to direct his steps"—is a
confession, not of sin, but of realized condition. Have we
ever made that confession in our own souls before God? If
we have, we know, and delight to know, that it is not within
man's power to arrange the course of his life. The test is,
have we the childlike attitude towards God; are we always
on the look-out for His supernatural working? Most of us
are rationalistic infidels; we never think that God is
supernatural at all. We rule out the miraculous and the
supernatural because it is not according to the outlook of
to-day.

Willing for the Loss of All Things?

But whatever was to my profit I now consider loss for the
sake of Christ. What is more, I consider everything a loss
compared to the surpassing greatness of knowing Christ
Jesus my Lord, for whose sake I have lost all things
(Philippians 3:7—8).

T o experience the loss of all things for anyone but
Jesus Christ is mental suicide. Read what Our Lord
said to the rich young ruler—"Sell whatsoever thou hast,
. . . and come, follow Me"—"Reduce yourself until you are
a mere conscious man, and then give that manhood to

Me;" and we read that "his countenance fell at the saying, and he went away sorrowful: for he was one that had great possessions." Do you possess a reputation as a Christian worker? That will be in the way when the Lord speaks to you. Are you rich in the consciousness that you are somebody spiritually? That will be in the way. You must first estimate and then experience the loss of all things and cast yourself on Jesus; then participation in godliness will be yours as it never has been.

MAY 11 _____

Intellectual Intemperance

Do not merely listen to the word, and so deceive yourselves. Do what it says *(James 1:22)*.

I ntellectual intemperance is a great snare to a saint. Bodily fasting is child's play compared to the determined fasting from the intellectual apprehension of the teachings of Jesus that goes beyond what we are living out. The characteristic of many spiritual people to-day is intellectual intemperance, fanatical intoxication with the things of God, wild exuberance, an unlikeness to the sanity of Jesus in the very ways of God. There is a danger in the enjoyment of the delights and the power that comes to us through Jesus Christ's salvation without lifting the life into keeping with His teaching, especially in spiritual people whose minds have never been disciplined and who wander off into all kinds of vagaries. That accounts for the distinction we find between spiritual sincerity and spiritual reality.

100

The Central Citadel for God

He is my loving God and my fortress, my stronghold and my deliverer, my shield, in whom I take refuge, who subdues peoples under me *(Psalm 144:2)*.

Who among you fears the LORD and obeys the word of his servant? Let him who walks in the dark, who has no light, trust in the name of the LORD and rely on his God *(Isaiah 50:10)*.

Watch the hard things Jesus says about father, mother, wife, children, our own life (see Luke 14:26); He says if we are going to follow Him, these must be on the outside of the central citadel. The central citadel must be God and God alone. When once we are willing to "do to death" our clinging to creatures, which in certain supreme calls comes between ourselves and God, Jesus says we will receive a hundredfold, because immediately we are rightly related to God. He can trust us with creature-relationships without fear of inordinateness.

Is the Cross an Offence?

For the message of the cross is foolishness to those who are perishing, but to us who are being saved it is the power of God. For it is written: "I will destroy the wisdom of the wise; the intelligence of the intelligent I will frustrate." Where is the wise man? Where is the scholar? Where is the philosopher of this age? Has not God made foolish the wisdom of the world? For since in the wisdom of God the world through its wisdom did not know him,

God was pleased through the foolishness of what was preached to save those who believe. Jews demand miraculous signs and Greeks look for wisdom, but we preach Christ crucified: a stumbling block to Jews and foolishness to Gentiles *(1 Corinthians 1:18–23)*.

R emember, it was not the "offscouring" that crucified Jesus; it was the highest reach of natural morality crucified Him. It is the refined, cultured, religious, moral people who refuse to sacrifice the natural for the spiritual. When once you get that thought, you understand the inveterate detestation of the Cross of Christ. Where are we with regard to this barter? Are we disciples of Jesus? Who is first, or what is first, in our lives? Who is the dominating personality that is dearer to us than life, ourselves or someone else? If it is someone else, who is it? It is only on such lines as these that we come to understand what Jesus meant when he said, "If any man would come after Me, let him deny himself." What He means is that He and what He stands for must be first.

MAY 14

Salvation Expressed in Bodily Life

I put this in human terms because you are weak in your natural selves. Just as you used to offer the parts of your body in slavery to impurity and to ever-increasing wickedness, so now offer them in slavery to righteousness leading to holiness *(Romans 6:19)*.

P aul is strong in urging us to realize what salvation means in our bodily lives; it means that we command our bodies to obey the new disposition. That is where you find the problems on the margins of the sanctified life. Paul argues in Romans 6:19, "You are perfectly adjusted to God on the inside by a perfect Saviour, but your members have been used as servants of the wrong disposition; now begin to make those same members obey the new disposition." As we go on, we find every place God brings us into is the means of enabling us to realize with growing joy that the life of Christ within is more than a match, not only for the enemy on the outside, but for the impaired body that comes between. Paul urges with passionate pleading, that we present our bodies a living sacrifice, and then realize, not presumptuously, but with slow, sure, overwhelming certainty that every command of Christ can be obeyed in our bodily life through the Atonement.

MAY 15 _____

Only God Understands Us

O LORD, you have searched me and you know me. You know when I sit and when I rise; you perceive my thoughts from afar. You discern my going out and my lying down; you are familiar with all my ways *(Psalm 139:1–3)*.

As long as we think we understand ourselves we are in a lamentable state of ignorance. The first dose of conviction of sin, or of the realization of what the Psalmist states—the unfathomable depths of our own souls—will put an end to that ignorance. The only One Who can redeem the human soul is the Lord Jesus Christ, and He has done it, and the Holy Spirit brings the realization of this to us experimentally. All this vast complex "me" which we cannot begin to understand, God knows completely, and through the Atonement He invades every part of our personality with His life. There is nothing simple in the human soul or in human life. The only simple thing is the relationship of the soul to Jesus Christ, and Paul says he fears lest we should be corrupted from that simplicity (2 Corinthians 11:3).

The Secret of True Fellowship

They devoted themselves to the apostles' teaching and to the fellowship, to the breaking of bread and of prayer *(Acts 2:42).*

And let us consider how we may spur one another on toward love and good deeds. Let us not give up meeting together, as some are in the habit of doing, but let us encourage one another—and all the more as you see the Day approaching *Hebrews 10:24–25).*

T hese passages indicate the main characteristic of Christianity in its working out, viz., the "together" aspect. Our Lord never inculcated an isolated holy life. Immediately we fix our eyes on our own whiteness, we lose sight of the purpose of Christianity. The Holy Spirit within a man makes him fix his eyes on his Lord, and on intense activity for other people. The individual man becomes so interdependent that he slowly loses his self-assertiveness until the oneness Jesus Christ prayed for is fulfilled. "If we walk in the light as God is in the light, . . . we have fellowship one with another." The Holy Spirit entering into the personal spirit instantly puts us into affinity with every other person in the light, hence Christian fellowship.

Christian fellowship has nothing to do with individual affinities, which are merely the husk of personality.

MAY 17 _____

The Gospel Creates Resentment

The sinful mind is hostile to God. It does not submit to God's law, nor can it do so (Romans 8:7).

T he Gospel does not present what the natural man wants, but what he needs, and the Gospel awakens an intense resentment as well as an intense craving. Why should the thing that upsets my peace be preached? I am living a simple, healthy, pagan life; my life does not spit through my creed and ridicule me; why should I be faced with an ideal which makes me know how tantalizingly short I come of it? At first the Gospel instead of being attractive is the opposite. The natural heart does not want the Gospel. We will take God's blessings and lovingkindnesses, but when it comes to the need of having the disposition of my soul altered, we find there is opposition at once. When we come down to close quarters and God's Spirit tells us we must give up the right to ourselves to Jesus Christ and let Him rule, then we understand what Paul meant when he said that the carnal mind, which resides in the heart, is *enmity* against God.

MAY 18 _____

Seeing Ourselves as God Sees Us

You, therefore, have no excuse, you who pass judgment on someone else, for at whatever point you judge the other, you are condemning yourself, because you who pass judgment do the same things *(Romans 2:1)*.

What we see to condemn in others is either the discernment of the Holy Ghost or the reflection of what we are capable of ourselves. We always notice how obtuse other people are before we notice how obtuse we are ourselves. If we see meanness in others, it is because we are mean ourselves. If we are inclined to be contemptuous over the fraud in others it is because we are frauds ourselves. We have to see ourselves as God sees us. When we do, it keeps us in the right place—"My God, was I ever like that to Thee, so opinionated and conceited, so set on my own ends, and so blind to myself?" If these things, which are most unpalatable, are not true, then Calvary is much ado about nothing.

MAY 19 _____

Christ Said, "For My Sake"

Then Jesus said to his disciples, "If anyone would come after me, he must deny himself and take up his cross and follow me. For whoever wants to save his life will lose it, but whoever loses his life for me will find it" *(Matthew 16:24–25)*.

Whenever the call is given for abandon to Jesus Christ, people say it is offensive and out of taste. The counterfeit of abandon is that misleading phrase "Christian service." I will spend myself for God, I will do anything and everything but the one thing he is asking me to do, viz., give up my right to myself to Him. We say, "But surely Christian service is a right thing." Immediately we begin to say that, we are off the track. It is the right *Person,* the Lord Jesus Christ, not the right thing. Don't stop short of the Lord Himself—*For My sake.* The great dominating recognition is that my personal self belongs to Jesus. When I receive the Holy Spirit, I receive not merely a possible oneness with Jesus Christ, but a real intense oneness with Him. The point is, will I surrender my individual life entirely to Him? It will mean giving up not only bad things, but things which are right and good (cf. Matt. 19:29–30). If you have to calculate what you are willing to give up for Jesus Christ, never say you love Him. Jesus Christ asks us to give up the best we have got to Him, our right to ourselves. Self-realization must be renounced in order that Jesus Christ may realize Himself in us.

MAY 20 _____

The Surgery of Providence

> When he came to his senses, he said, "How many of my father's hired men have food to spare, and here I am starving to death! I will set out and go back to my father and say to him: Father, I have sinned against heaven and against you. I am no longer worthy to be called your son; make me like one of your hired men." So he got up and went to his father *(Luke 15:17–20).*

There is no pain on earth to equal the pain of wounded self-love. Unrequited love is bad enough, but wounded self-love is the cruelest thing to a human being because it shifts the whole foundations of the life. The prodigal son had his self-love wounded; he was full of shame and indignation because he had sunk to such a level. ". . . and I perish with hunger!" There was remorse, but no repent-

107

ance yet, no thought of his father. "I will arise and go to my father and will say unto him, I have sinned . . . and am no more worthy to be called thy son: . . . And he arose, and came to his father." That is repentance. The surgery of providence had done its work; he was no longer deluded about himself. A repentant soul is never allowed to remain long without being gripped by the love of God.

"Man, what is this, and why art thou despairing?
God shall forgive thee all but thy despair."

Let the surgery of providence drive you straight to God.

MAY 21 _____

Spiritual Beauty

And the child grew and became strong; he was filled with wisdom, and the grace of God was upon him *(Luke 2:40)*.

The presentation of true Christian experience brings us face to face with spiritual beauty, a beauty which can never be forced or imitated, because it is a manifestation from within of a simple relationship to God that is being worked out all the time. There is nothing simple saving a man's relation to God in Christ (2 Corinthians 11:3), and that relationship must never be allowed to be complicated. Our Lord's childhood expresses this spiritual beauty— "And the child grew, and waxed strong, becoming full of wisdom." "And Jesus advanced in wisdom and age" (Luke 2:40, 52 R.V. marg.). Jesus Christ developed in the way that God intended human beings to develop, and He exhibited the kind of life we ought to live when we have been born from above.

The Knowledge of Good and Evil

When the woman saw that the fruit of the tree was good for food and pleasing to the eye, and also desirable for gaining wisdom, she took some and ate it *(Genesis 3:6)*.

Modern teaching implies that we must be grossly experienced before we can be of any use in the world. That is not true. Jesus Christ understood as no one else has done, but He never ate of the tree of knowledge of good and evil. Our Lord knew good and evil by the life that was in Him; and God intended that man's knowledge of evil should come in the same way as it came to Our Lord, viz., through the rigorous integrity of obedience to God. It is only when a man is delivered from sin that the Spirit of God begins to give him an understanding of what sin is. When a man is convicted of sin he knows how terrific the havoc is that sin has wrought in him; he knows with what a mighty salvation he has been visited by God; but it is only by obedience to the Holy Spirit that he begins to know what an awful thing sin is.

The Hope of the Otherworldly

Then I saw a new heaven and a new earth, for the first heaven and the first earth had passed away, and there was no longer any sea. I saw the Holy City, the new

Jerusalem, coming down out of heaven from God, prepared as a bride beautifully dressed for her husband. And I heard a loud voice from the throne saying, "Now the dwelling of God is with men, and he will live with them. They will be his people, and God himself will be with them and be their God. He will wipe every tear from their eyes. There will be no more death or mourning or crying or pain, for the old order of things has passed away." He who was seated on the throne said, "I am making everything new!" Then he said, "Write this down, for these words are trustworthy and true" *(Revelation 21:1–5).*

T he otherworldly person has the belief that everything hoped for or imagined or dreamed about will be absolutely fulfilled and more than fulfilled. This hope runs all through the poetry of the world; it is born of God, but the world does not allow it to be fulfilled in God's way. The saint has not only the vision of the poet, but he submits to God's way of fulfillment, viz., by the removal of sin, the salvation of sinners, and the sanctification of believers. The danger comes from having barren brains. We have no business to have barren brains. We ought to use our brains until they are thoroughly furnished on God's line. We are tired nowadays of preaching about a future heaven, and have gone to the other extreme and deal only with what we call the practical. We rob ourselves of the tremendous unfathomable certainty that everything God has promised will come to pass. When a Christian has hold of that hope he purifies himself "even as He is pure." Nothing can disconcert or upset him because he knows it is only an episode.

Ignorant Innocence

"For from within, out of men's hearts, come evil thoughts, sexual immorality, theft, murder, adultery, greed, malice, deceit, lewdness, envy, slander, arrogance and folly. All these evils come from inside and make a man 'unclean'" *(Mark 7:21–23)*.

E very child born of natural generation is innocent, but it is the innocence of ignorance. Naturally we are in an impaired state, and when our innocence is turned into knowledge we find to our humiliation how tremendously impaired it is. It is the ignorant innocence of determinedly being without the knowledge of God. It is safer to trust God's revelation than our own innocence. Jesus Christ is either the supreme Authority on the human heart, or He is not worth listening to, and He said: "From within out of the heart of man proceed . . ." and then comes that very ugly catalogue. He did not say: "Into the human heart these things are injected," but "from within out of the heart of men, . . . all these evil things proceed." If we trust our innocent ignorance to secure us, it is likely that there will be as life goes on a burst up into our conscious life from underneath which will reveal to us that we are uncommonly like what Jesus Christ says.

True Repentance

"Return, faithless people; I will cure you of backsliding."
"Yes, we will come to you, for you are the LORD our

God. Surely the idolatrous commotion on the hills and mountains is a deception; surely in the LORD our God is the salvation of Israel. From our youth shameful gods have consumed the fruits of our fathers' labor—their flocks and herds, their sons and daughters. Let us lie down in our shame, and let our disgrace cover us. We have sinned against the LORD our God, both we and our fathers; from our youth till this day we have not obeyed the LORD our God" *(Jeremiah 3:22–25)*.

R epentance means to feel the sorrow which produces new life. Repentance means the miracle of never being again what I was before. It is not sorrow for sin only, but the kind of sorrow that puts an end for ever to the thing over which I sorrow. The only truly repentant man is the holy man. Repentance is spoken of as a gift; it does not spring naturally from the human heart; it is the presence in the human heart of something that springs from the ground of Redemption, and has all the power of a totally new life. Most of us only know remorse, which means I am disgusted with myself; the rarest miracle of God's grace is repentance which by the grace of God turns us into the opposite of what we were.

MAY 26 ——————————————————————

The Cleansing of the Blood

But if we walk in the light, as he is in the light, we have fellowship with one another, and the blood of Jesus, his Son, purifies us from all sin *(1 John 1:7)*.

C leansing from all sin is far deeper than we can be conscious of: it is cleansing from all sin in the sight of God. The Holy Spirit applies the Atonement to the unconscious realm as well as the conscious, and cleansing from all sin refers to the tremendously profound understanding of sin which only the Holy Ghost has. "If we walk in the light as God is in the light," i.e., with nothing to hide, nothing folded up, then there comes the amazing revelation—"the blood of Jesus Christ His Son *cleanseth us from all sin.*" We are not cleansed more and more from sin; when we are in the light as God is in the light, walking in it, we *are* cleansed from all sin so that God Almighty can see nothing to censure. In our consciousness it works with a keen poignant knowledge of what sin is. The supernatural revelation of Jesus Christ's salvation is that we stand in God's sight free from sin, not in our consciousness; the thing we are conscious of is walking in the light with nothing to hide. As long as we walk there, God sees nothing to censure because the life of His Son is working out in every particular.

MAY 27 _____

Progressive Outworking of Holiness

Therefore, my dear friends, as you have always obeyed—not only in my presence, but now much more in my absence—continue to work out your salvation with fear and trembling, for it is God who works in you to will and to act according to his good purpose *(Philippians 2:12–13).*

T he great need to-day amongst those of us who profess sanctification is the patience and ability to work out the holiness of God in every detail of the life. When we are first adjusted to God it is on the great big general lines; then the Holy Spirit educates us down to the

113

scruple; He makes us sensitive to things we never thought of before. No matter what our experience may be, we must beware of the curse of being stationary; we have to go on and on in the holy life until we manifest the disposition God has given us in every detail of our lives. The disposition of Jesus enables us to keep all the commandments of God, not some of them.

MAY 28 _____

The Divine Scrutiny

Therefore judge nothing before the appointed time; wait till the Lord comes. He will bring to light what is hidden in darkness and will expose the motives of men's hearts. At that time each will receive his praise from God (1 Corinthians 4:5).

Are we willing to let God scrutinize us, or are we doing the worst of all things, trying to justify ourselves? People say if they are walking up to the light they have, meaning the light of conscience, they are all right. We may be consciously free from sin, but we are not justified on that account; we may be walking in all the light of conscience, but we are not justified on that account either. We are only justified in the sight of God through the Atonement of Jesus Christ at work in our inner life. God grant we may let His searching scrutiny go through our hearts and spirits until there is nothing that God has not searched. We cannot cabin and confine our lives; there is a purpose in them that is in God's keeping and we know nothing of, but which God will fulfill if we let His tremendous scrutiny go through us and rightly relate us to Himself.

Our Attitude to the Worldly

> Do you not know that the wicked will not inherit the kingdom of God? Do not be deceived: Neither the sexually immoral nor idolaters nor adulterers nor male prostitutes nor homosexual offenders nor thieves nor the greedy nor drunkards nor slanderers nor swindlers will inherit the kingdom of God. And that is what some of you were. But you were washed, you were sanctified, you were justified in the name of the Lord Jesus Christ and by the Spirit of God. "Everything is permissible for me"—but not everything is beneficial. "Everything is permissible for me"—but I will not be mastered by anything. "Food for the stomach and the stomach for food"—but God will destroy them both. The body is not meant for sexual immorality, but for the Lord, and the Lord for the body *(1 Corinthians 6:9–13).*

B y "Worldly" understand the system of men and women in any particular time who order their religion, their business, and their social life without any concern as to how it affects Jesus Christ.

We must distinguish between immoral conduct inside and outside the Christian community. We must sternly and unbendingly and unsympathetically rebuke immoral conduct inside the Christian community; outside the Christian community we must bear the shame and humiliation of contact with men vicariously, as Jesus did, that by our lives we may win them to God. Jesus Christ lived amongst the publicans and sinners, people who were guilty of the things Paul condemns (see Matthew 11:19). The condemnation lies in having anything to do with these things inside the Christian community. It is easy to denounce wrong in the world; anyone without a spark of grace can do that, while all the time we may be allowing worldly things in our own lives.

_____

Conviction of Sin in the Saint

"Woe to me!" I cried, "I am ruined! For I am a man of unclean lips, and I live among a people of unclean lips, and my eyes have seen the King, the LORD Almighty" *(Isaiah 6:5)*.

C onscience is rarely aroused by conviction of sin to begin with; all we can stand until we are saints is conviction of having done wrong things. Sin is much more than an act; sin is a disposition, and only a saint is able to stand conviction of sin. If God gave us conviction of sin, without our having an experience of Redemption, we should be driven insane. The terror of the conviction of sin aroused by the Holy Spirit is that a man knows that God dare not forgive him. It is because we have missed altogether the miracle of the forgiveness of God that we talk so glibly about it—"God is love, therefore of course, He will forgive sin." We easily forgive ourselves; we get disgusted for a while and then say—To know all is to forgive all. To know all is to be able to forgive nothing. God cannot forgive unless He does so on a basis that goes deeper than sin, viz., the basis of Redemption, which means the total alteration of the sinner. If God does not forgive the sinner out of a man, His forgiveness is a farce; and He is not justified in forgiving. The only standard for forgiveness is what it cost God to forgive. It cost Him Calvary. It cost God everything that the Divine nature could give to be able to say, "Thy sins be forgiven thee."

MAY 31 _____

Righteousness That Exceeds

"For I tell you that unless your righteousness surpasses that of the Pharisees and the teachers of the law, you will certainly not enter the kingdom of heaven" *(Matthew 5:20).*

Our righteousness has to be in excess of the righteousness of the man whose external conduct is blameless according to the law—what does that produce? Despair straightaway. When we hear Jesus say "Blessed are the pure in heart," our answer, if we are awake is, "My God, how am I going to be pure in heart? If ever I am to be blameless down to the deepest recesses of my intentions, You must do something mighty in me." That is exactly what Jesus Christ came to do. He did not come to *tell us* to be holy, but to *make* us holy, undeserving of censure in the sight of God. If any man or woman gets there it is by the sheer supernatural grace of God.

JUNE 1 _____

The Final Victory

See, the Sovereign Lord comes with power, and his arm rules for him. See, his reward is with him, and his recompense accompanies him *(Isaiah 40:10).*

117

"Men of Galilee," they said, "why do you stand here looking into the sky? This same Jesus, who has been taken from you into heaven, will come back in the same way you have seen him go into heaven" *(Acts 1:11)*.

The remarkable thing in the record of the Ages that have been, and that are, and that are going to be, is that each Age ends in apparent disaster. The saint alone knows by spiritual intuition that "He doeth all things well"; he knows that God reigns, and that the clouds are but the dust of his Father's feet, and he has no need to fear. He feels assured that these catastrophic occurrences are but incidental, and that a higher peace and a purer character are to be the permanent result. He knows that "this same Jesus," who trod this earth with naked feet, "and wrought with human hands the creed of creeds," is coming again, visibly and blessedly coming to earth again, when the petition will be fulfilled, *"Thy kingdom come."* All that men have ever dreamed of Utopias and of Golden Ages will fade into foolish fancies beside the wonder of that blessed Age, that blessed period of Christ's reign among men.

JUNE 2 _____

Keep True to the Light

When Jesus told them, "You are going to have the light just a little while longer. Walk while you have the light, before darkness overtakes you. The man who walks in the dark does not know where he is going. Put your trust in the light while you have it, so that you may become sons of light." When he had finished speaking, Jesus left and hid himself from them *(John 12:35–36)*.

118

The discernment of God's call does not come in every moment of life, but only in rare moments, the moments Our Lord spoke of as "the light." We have to remain true to what we see in those moments; if we do not we will put back God's purpose in our lives. The undercurrent of regret arises when we confer with those who have not heard the call of God, and if we listen to them we get into darkness. The life of Abraham is an illustration of two things: of unreserved surrender to God, and of God's complete possession of a child of His for His own highest ends.

JUNE 3 _____

Afraid of Poverty?

"Therefore I tell you, do not worry about your life, what you will eat or drink; or about your body, what you will wear. Is not life more important than food, and the body more important than clothes? Look at the birds of the air; they do not sow or reap or store away in barns, and yet your heavenly Father feeds them. Are you not much more valuable than they? Who of you by worrying can add a single hour to his life? And why do you worry about clothes? See how the lilies of the field grow. They do not labor or spin. Yet I tell you that not even Solomon in all his splendor was dressed like one of these. If that is how God clothes grass of the field, which is here today and tomorrow is thrown into the fire, will he not much more clothe you, O you of little faith? So do not worry, saying, 'What shall we eat?' or 'What shall we drink?' or 'What shall we wear?' For the pagans run after all these things, and your heavenly Father knows that you need them. But seek first his kingdom and his righteousness,

119

and all these things will be given to you as well. Therefore do not worry about tomorrow, for tomorrow will worry about itself. Each day has enough trouble of its own" *(Matthew 6:25—34)*.

Today we are so afraid of poverty that we never dream of doing anything that might involve us in being poor. We are out of the running of the medieval monks who took on the vow of poverty. Many of us are poor, but none of us chooses to be. Our attitude is that if we are extravagant, a rainy day will come for which we have not laid up. You cannot lay up for a rainy day and justify it in the light of Jesus Christ's teaching. We are not Christians at heart; we don't believe in the wisdom of God, but only in our own. We go in for insurance and economy and speculation, everything that makes us secure in our own wisdom.

JUNE 4 _____

The Two-edged Sword

Take the helmet of salvation and the sword of the Spirit, which is the word of God *(Ephesians 6:17)*.

The word of God is living and active. Sharper than any double-edged sword, it penetrates even to dividing soul and spirit, joints and marrow; it judges the thoughts and attitudes of the heart *(Hebrews 4:12)*,

And take . . . the sword of the Spirit, which is the word of God." When I have been using "the sword of the Spirit" in a spirit of indignation against another, it is a terrible experience to find the sword suddenly wrested out of my hand and laid about me personally by God. Let your personal experience of the work of God's Spirit instruct you at the foot of Calvary; let the light of God riddle you through; then you will never use the word of God to another, never turn the light of God on him, without fear and trembling. "For the word of God is living, and active, and sharper than any two-edged sword, . . ." The word of God is the sword that cuts first in me and then in others. The truth of God can never be escaped from by those who utter it—"Thou therefore that teaches, *teaches thou not thyself? Thou that preachest a man should not steal, dost thou steal?*"

JUNE 5 _____

The Discipline of Human Nature

And in him you too are being built together to become a dwelling in which God lives by his Spirit *(Ephesians 2:22)*.

Through these he has given us his very great and precious promises, so that through them you may participate in the divine nature and escape the corruption in the world caused by evil desires. For this very reason, make every effort to add to your faith goodness; and to goodness, knowledge; and to knowledge, self-control; and to self-control, perseverance; and to perseverance, godliness; and to godliness, brotherly kindness; and to brotherly kindness, love *(2 Peter 1:4–7)*.

We are not delivered from human nature; human nature was created by God, not by the devil; it is impaired, and enfeebled, but it is not sinful. The first creation retains the remnants of God's handiwork; re-creation is the building of a spiritual habitation, "an habitation of God," and all our effort is to be spent in disciplining the natural life in obedience to the new creation wrought in us through the Spirit. If I refuse to make my natural life spiritual by the slow process of obedience, my religious profession becomes a disgusting hypocrisy. Any attempt to build on the natural virtues will ultimately outrage the grace of God, whereas dependence on God means the successful working of God's grace in me. "I do not make void the grace of God," said Paul.

JUNE 6 _____

The Test of Fruit

> Seeing a fig tree by the road, he went up to it but found nothing on it except leaves. Then he said to it, "May you never bear fruit again!" Immediately the tree withered *(Matthew 21:19)*.

> "This is to my Father's glory, that you bear much fruit, showing yourselves to be my disciples" *(John 15:8)*.

L eaves of a tree are *a* fruit, but not *the* fruit; they are for the nourishment of the tree itself; that is why in the autumn they push off and sink into the ground where they become disintegrated and are taken into the root again. The fruit proper is never for the tree itself; it is for the husbandman. Woe be to the man who mistakes leaves for fruit! The reason Our Lord cursed the barren fig tree was because it stood as a symbol of leaves being proudly mistaken for fruit (see Matthew 21:19). When we mistake what we do for the fruit, we are deluded; what tells is not what we do, but what is produced by what we do.

The Secret of Reality

"No one can come to me unless the Father who sent me draws him, and I will raise him up at the last day. It is written in the Prophets: 'They will all be taught by God.' Everyone who listens to the Father and learns from him comes to me. No one has seen the Father except the one who is from God; only he has seen the Father. I tell you the truth, he who believes has everlasting life. I am the bread of life. Your forefathers ate the manna in the desert, yet they died. But here is the bread that comes down from heaven, which a man may eat and not die. I am the living bread that came down from heaven. If a man eats of this bread, he will live forever. This bread is my flesh, which I will give for the life of the world" *(John 6:44–51).*

T here is no delusion in Christian experience; it begins outside me by creating in me an enormous craving, akin to thirst or to hunger. This craving is created by the reality of the Redemption, not by my penetrating insight, but by what Jesus calls "the drawing of the Father" (John 6:44). I am brought face to face with Jesus Christ and made to see that God has promised to give the Holy Spirit to them that ask Him. I ask, and I receive by believing the gift of the Holy Spirit, i.e., I receive a complete satisfaction.

No Compromise With Mammon

"No one can serve two masters. Either he will hate the one and love the other, or he will be devoted to the one and despise the other. You cannot serve both God and Money" *(Matthew 6:24).*

"No man can serve two masters";
"Ye cannot serve God and mammon."

Have we allowed these inexorable decisions of Our Lord to have their powerful way in our thinking? The line of detachment runs all through Our Lord's teaching: You cannot be good and bad at the same time; you cannot serve God and make your own out of the service; you cannot make "honesty is the best policy" a motive, because immediately you do, you cease to be honest. There is to be only one consideration, a right relationship with God, and see that that relationship is never dimmed. Never compromise with the spirit of mammon. It is easy to associate mammon only with sordid things; mammon is the system of civilized life which organizes itself without any consideration of God (cf. Luke 16:15).

JUNE 9 _____

The School of Calvary

For I resolved to know nothing while I was with you except Jesus Christ and him crucified *(1 Corinthians 2:2).*

The call to preach is not because I have a special gift, or because Jesus has sanctified me, but that I have had a glimpse of God's meaning in the Cross, and life can never be the same again. The passion of Paul's preaching is the suffering of God Almighty exhibited in the Cross of Christ. Many who are working for God ought to be learning in the School of Calvary. Paul says—"I determined not to know any thing among you, save Jesus Christ, and Him crucified,"—not myself crucified with Christ, that is a mere *et cetera;* the one Figure left is Jesus Christ, and His Cross.

God's Amazing Treatment of His Penitent Child

So he got up and went to his father. But while he was still a long way off, his father saw him and was filled with compassion for him; he ran to his son, threw his arms around him and kissed him. The son said to him, "Father, I have sinned against heaven and against you. I am no longer worthy to be called your son." But the father said to his servants, "Quick! Bring the best robe and put it on him. Put a ring on his finger and sandals on his feet. Bring the fattened calf and kill it. Let's have a feast and celebrate.. For this son of mine was dead and is alive again; he was lost and is found." So they began to celebrate. Meanwhile, the older son was in the field. When he came near the house, he heard music and dancing. So he called one of the servants and asked him what was going on. "Your brother has come," he replied, "and your father has killed the fattened calf because he has him back safe and sound." The older brother became angry and refused to go in. So his father went out and pleaded with him. But he answered his father, "Look! All these years I've been slaving for you and never disobeyed your orders. Yet you never gave me even a young goat so I could celebrate with my friends. But when this son of yours who has squandered your property with prostitutes comes home, you kill the fattened calf for him!" "My son," the father said, "you are always with me, and everything I have is yours. But we had to celebrate and be glad, because this brother of yours was dead and is alive again; he was lost and is found" *(Luke 15:20–32)*.

T he presentation given in the parable is that the father makes no conditions when the prodigal comes back, neither does he bring home to him any remembrance of the far country—the elder brother does that; it is the revelation of the unfathomable, unalterable, amazing love of God. We would feel much happier in our back-slidden condition if we knew that our backsliding had altered God, but we know that immediately we come back we will find Him exactly the same, and that is one of the things that keeps men from coming back. If God would only be angry with us and demand an apology, it would be a gratification to us; when we have done wrong we like to be lashed for it. God never lashes. Jesus does not represent the father as saying, "You have been so wicked that I cannot take you back as my son, I will make you a servant," but as saying, "Bring forth quickly the best robe and put it on him; and put a ring on his hand, and shoes on his feet—and bring the fatted calf, and kill it, and let us eat, and make merry; for this my son was dead, and is alive again; he was lost, and is found."

JUNE 11 _____

Discerning God's Point of View

So we fix our eyes not on what is seen, but on what is unseen. For what is seen is temporary, but what is unseen is eternal *(2 Corinthians 4:18)*.

T here never was anyone who did not have one moment when all the machinery tumbled away and he saw the meaning of his life. God pays not the remotest attention to our civilized cultures and our attitudes to things, because that is not what we are here for. We are here for one thing—to glorify God. That is where we join issue with the Lord Jesus Christ to-day, and we look at every other thing as life—"What shall we eat? What shall we drink? Wherewithal shall we be clothed?" Our Lord came for one purpose only, to reveal God, and to get men to be spiritually real.

JUNE 12 _____

The Divine Estimate of Life

"At that time the kingdom of heaven will be like ten virgins who took their lamps and went out to meet the bridegroom. Five of them were foolish and five were wise. The foolish ones took their lamps but did not take any oil with them. The wise, however, took oil in jars along with their lamps. The bridegroom was a long time in coming, and they all became drowsy and fell asleep. At midnight the cry rang out: 'Here's the bridegroom! Come out to meet him!' Then all the virgins woke up and trimmed their lamps. The foolish ones said to the wise, 'Give us some of your oil; our lamps are going out.' 'No,' they replied, 'there may not be enough for both us and you. Instead, go to those who sell oil and buy some for yourselves.' But while they were on their way to buy the oil, the bridegroom arrived. The virgins who were ready went in with him to the wedding banquet. And the door was shut. Later the others also came, 'Sir! Sir!' they said. 'Open the door for us!' But he replied, 'I tell you the truth, I don't know you.' Therefore keep watch, because you do not know the day or the hour. Again, it will be like a man going on a journey, who called his servants and entrusted his property to them. To one he gave five talents of money, to another two talents, and to another one talent, each according to his ability. Then he went on his journey. The man who had received the five talents went at once and put his money to work and gained five more. So also, the one with the two talents gained two more. But the man who had received the one talent went off, dug a hole in the ground and hid his master's money. After a long time the master of those servants returned and settled accounts with them. The man who had received the five talents brought the other five. 'Master,' he said, 'you entrusted me with five talents. See, I have gained five more.' His master replied, 'Well done, good and faithful servant! You have been faithful with a few things: I will put you in charge of many things. Come and share your master's happiness!' The man with the two talents also came. 'Master,' he said, 'you entrusted me with two talents; see, I have gained two more.' His master replied, 'Well done, good and faithful servant! You have been faithful with a few things; I will put you in charge of many things. Come and share your master's happiness!' Then the man who had received the one talent came. 'Master,' he said, 'I knew that you are a hard man, harvesting where you have not sown and gathering where you have not scattered seed. So I was afraid and went out and hid your talent in the ground. See, here is what belongs to you.' His master replied, 'You wicked, lazy servant! So you knew that I harvest where I have not sown and gather where I have not scattered seed? Well then, you should have put my money on deposit with the bankers, so that when I returned I would have received it back with interest. Take the talent from him and give it to the one who has the ten talents. For everyone who has will be given more, and he will have an abundance. Whoever does not have, even what he has will be taken from him. And throw that worthless servant outside, into the darkness, where there will be weeping and gnashing of teeth" *(Matthew 25:1–30)*.

The parable of the ten virgins reveals that it is fatal from our Lord's standpoint to live this life without preparation for the life to come. That is not the exegesis; it is the obvious underlying principle.

The parable of the talents is our Lord's statement with regard to the danger of leaving undone the work of a lifetime.

And the description of the last judgment is the picture of genuine astonishment on the part of both the losers and the gainers of what they had never once thought about.

JUNE 13 _____

Strength for the Battle

For our struggle is not against flesh and blood, but against the rulers, against the authorities, against the powers of this dark world and against the spiritual forces of evil in the heavenly realms *(Ephesians 6:12)*.

Or else let them come to me for refuge; let them make peace with me, yes, let them make peace with me *(Isaiah 27:5)*.

We must learn to draw on the supernatural power of God, realizing that our enemies are supernatural, not natural; that our battling is not with difficult circumstances; it is altogether a battling that God is waging for us if we will draw on the supernatural forces. A Christian life lived on any other plane is an impossible life. If we stop drawing, down we go; worry breaks the mind, trouble crushes the spirit, and calamity annihilates the strength of the life, and written over it is God's curse. No Christian has a right to be weak in God's strength.

The Weapon of All Prayer

And pray in the Spirit on all occasions with all kinds of prayers and requests. With this in mind, be alert and always keep on praying for all the saints *(Ephesians 6:18)*.

T he fundamental basis of the human will deep down is inclined towards God, and prayer works wonders fundamentally. The prayer of the feeblest saint on earth who lives in the Spirit and keeps right with God is a terror to Satan. The very powers of darkness are paralyzed by prayer; no spiritualistic seance can succeed in the presence of a humble praying saint. No wonder Satan tries to keep our minds fussy in active work till we cannot think in prayer. It is a vital necessity for Christians to think along the lines on which they pray. The philosophy of prayer is that prayer is *the* work.

The Stronger One

The One enthroned in heaven laughs; the LORD scoffs at them *(Psalm 2:4)*.

S atan is overcome not in a battle, but by the easy might of a power greater than his own coming upon him, and that power is none other than our Lord Himself. Every now and again when you look at life from a certain angle it seems as if evil and wrong and legalized iniquity are having it all their own way and you feel that everything must go to pieces; but it doesn't; around it is the sovereignty of God, "Hitherto shalt thou come, but no further." Blessed be the Name of God, evil shall not ultimately triumph! Let evil do its worst, let the arrogance of self-interested iniquity in all shapes and forms surge as it may, but "He that sitteth in the heavens shall laugh: the Lord shall have them in derision." The Spirit of God shatters every power of the world, the flesh and the devil, every power of sin and the domination of Satan.

JUNE 16 _____

Divine Concealing and Human Curiosity

It is the glory of God to conceal a matter; to search out a matter is the glory of kings *(Proverbs 25:2)*.

I t is the glory of God to conceal a thing." God will not have us come with an impatient curiosity. Moral or intellectual or spiritual insanity must result if we push down barriers which God has placed before our spiritual progress is fit for the revelation. This is a day of intolerant inquisitiveness. Men will not wait for the slow, steady, majestic way of the Son of God; they try to enter in by this door and that door. "And one of the elders saith unto me, Weep not: behold, the Lion that is of the tribe of Judah, the Root of David, hath overcome, to open the book and the seven seals thereof" (Revelation 5:5). The barriers are placed by a Holy God, and He has told us clearly—"Not

131

that way." God grant we may accept His clouds and mysteries, and be led into His inner secrets by obedient trust.

JUNE 17 _____

Misjudging God's Ways

Light is shed upon the righteous and joy on the upright in heart. Rejoice in the LORD, you who are righteous, and praise his holy name *(Psalm 97:11–12),*

I f we go on obeying God, we shall find that "light is sown for the righteous." We are so impatient—"I thought God's purpose was to make me full of happiness and joy." It is, but it is happiness and joy from God's standpoint, not from ours. God always ignores the present perfection for the ultimate perfection. We bring God to the bar of our judgment and say hard things about Him— "Why does God bring thunderclouds and disasters when we want green pastures and still waters?" Bit by bit we find, behind the clouds, the Father's feet; behind the lightning, an abiding day that has no night; behind the thunder a still small voice that comforts with a comfort that is unspeakable.

JUNE 18 _____

Treasures of Darkness

"I will give you the treasures of darkness, riches stored in secret places, so that you may know that I am the LORD, the God of Israel, who calls you by name" *(Isaiah 45:3).*

I t is the glory of God to conceal His treasures in embarrassments, i.e., in things that involve us in difficulty. "I will give thee the treasures of darkness." We would never have suspected that treasures were hidden there, and in order to get them we have to go through things that involve us in perplexity. There is nothing more wearying to the eye than perpetual sunshine, and the same is true spiritually. The valley of the shadow gives us time to reflect, and we learn to praise God for the valley because in it our soul was restored in its communion with God. God gives us a new revelation of His kindness in the valley of the shadow. What are the days and the experiences that have furthered us most? The days of green pastures, of absolute ease? No, they have their value; but the days that have furthered us most in character are the days of stress and cloud.

JUNE 19 _____

The Only Answer

The next day John saw Jesus coming toward him and said, "Look, the Lamb of God, who takes away the sin of the world!" *(John 1:29).*

W here are we in regard to the personal experience of the baptism of the Holy Ghost? If Jesus Christ had said to us, "All you need to do is to be as holy as you can, overcome sin as far as you can, and I will overlook the rest," no intelligent man under heaven would accept such a salvation. But He says—"Be ye perfect"; "Love your enemies"; "Be so pure that lust is an impossibility." Instantly every heart calls back, "My God, who is sufficient

133

for these things?" Oceans of penitential tears, mountains of good works, all powers and energy sink down till they are under the feet of the Lord Jesus, and, incarnate in John the Baptist, they all point to Him—"Behold the Lamb of God, which taketh away the sins of the world."

JUNE 20 _____

Complete Deliverance Possible

And God is able to make all grace abound to you, so that in all things at all times, having all that you need, you will abound in every good work. As it is written: "He has scattered abroad his gifts to the poor; his righteousness endures forever." Now he who supplies seed to the sower and bread for food will also supply and increase your store of seed and will enlarge the harvest of your righteousness. You will be made rich in every way so that you can be generous on every occasion, and through us your generosity will result in thanksgiving to God *(2 Corinthians 9:8–11)*.

I f Jesus Christ cannot deliver from sin, if He cannot adjust us perfectly to God as He says he can; if He cannot fill us with the Holy Ghost until there is nothing that can ever appeal again in sin or the world or the flesh, then He has misled us. But blessed be the Name of God, He can! He can so purify, so indwell, so merge with Himself, that only the things that appeal to Him appeal to you. To all other appeals there is the sentence of death; you have nothing to answer. When you come amongst those whose morality and uprightness crown them the lord of their own lives, there is no affinity with you, and they leave you alone.

The Rest of Patience and Faith

This is what the Sovereign LORD, the Holy One of Israel, says: "In repentance and rest is your salvation, in quietness and trust is your strength, but you would have none of it" *(Isaiah 30:15)*.

T o wait upon God is the perfection of activity. We are told to "rest in the Lord," not to rust. We talk of resting in the Lord but it is often only a pious expression; in the Bible, resting in the Lord is the patience of godly confidence. "In returning and rest shall ye be saved; . . . But ye said, No, for we will flee upon horses;" i.e., we will take the initiative. When we take the initiative we put our wits on the throne; we do not worship God.

"Wait Only Upon God"

Find rest, O my soul, in God alone; my hope comes from him *(Psalm 62:5)*.

I s silent prayer to us an experience of waiting upon God, or is it a "cotton wool" experience, utterly dim and dark? A time which we simply endure until it is over? If you want discerning vision about anything, you have to make an effort and call in your wandering attention. Mental woolgathering can be stopped immediately the will is roused. Prayer is an effort of will, and the great battle in prayer is the overcoming of mental woolgathering. We put things down to the devil when we should put them down to our own inability to concentrate. "My soul, wait thou only

135

upon God," i.e, "Pull yourself together and be silent unto God."

Through the Cross to ... ?

> But whatever was to my profit I now consider loss for the sake of Christ. What is more, I consider everything a loss compared to the surpassing greatness of knowing Christ Jesus my Lord, for whose sake I have lost all things. I consider them rubbish, that I may gain Christ and be found in him, not having a righteousness of my own that comes from the law, but that which is through faith in Christ—the righteousness that comes from God and is by faith. I want to know Christ and the power of his resurrection and the fellowship of sharing in his sufferings, becoming like him in his death *(Philippians 3:7– 10)*.

How much more is there to know, after sanctification? Everything! Before sanctification we know nothing, we are simply put in the place of knowing; that is, we are led *up* to the Cross; in santification we are led *through* the Cross—for what purpose? For a life of outpouring service to God. The characteristic of a saint after identification with the death of Jesus is that he is brought down from the ineffable glory of the heavenly places into the valley to be crushed and broken in service for God. We are here with no right to ourselves, for no spiritual blessing for ourselves; we are here for one purpose only—to be made servants of God as Jesus was. Have we as saints allowed our minds to be brought face to face with this great truth?

_____

The Miracle of Restoration

"I will repay you for the years the locusts have eaten—
the great locust and the young locust, the other locusts
and the locust swarm—my great army that I sent among
you" *(Joel 2:25)*.

Many a sensitive soul has been driven into insanity
through anguish of mind because he has never
realized what Jesus Christ came to do, and all the asylums
in the world will never touch them in the way of healing; the
only thing that will is the realization of what the death of
Jesus means, viz., that the damage we have done may be
repaired through the efficacy of His Cross. Jesus Christ has
atoned for all, and He can make it good in us, not only as a
gift but by a participation on our part. The miracle of the
grace of God is that He can make the past as though it had
never been; He can "restore the years that the locust hath
eaten, the cankerworm, and the caterpillar, and the
palmerworm."

_____

The Mystery of His Desolation

And at the ninth hour Jesus cried out in a loud voice,
"Eloi, Eloi, lama sabacthani?"—which means, "My
God, my God, why have you forsaken me?" *(Mark
15:34)*.

But we see Jesus, who was made a little lower than the
angels, now crowned with glory and honor because he

137

suffered death, so that by the grace of God he might taste death for everyone *(Hebrews 2:9).*

T he cry on the Cross, "My God, My God, why hast Thou forsaken Me?" is unfathomable to us. The only ones—and I want to say this very deliberately—the only ones who come near the threshold of understanding the cry of Jesus are not the martyrs; they knew that God had not forsaken them, His presence was so wonderful; not the lonely missionaries who are killed or forsaken, they experience exultant joy, for God is with them when men forsake them: the only ones who come near the threshold of understanding the experience of Godforsakenness are men like Cain—"My punishment is greater than I can bear"; men like Esau, "an exceeding bitter cry"; men like Judas. Jesus Christ knew and tasted to a fuller depth than any man could ever taste what it is to be separated from God by sin.

JUNE 26 ⸻⸻⸻⸻⸻⸻⸻⸻⸻⸻⸻⸻

Our Magnanimous God

"He causes his sun to rise on the evil and the good, and sends rain on the righteous and the unrighteous" *(Matthew 5:45).*

I n the first place, our great God's blessings fall, like His rain, on evil and good alike. The great blessings of health, genius, prosperity, all come from His overflowing grace, and not from the condition of the character of the recipients. For instance, if health were a sign that a man is right with God, we should lose all distinction as to what a good character is, for many bad men enjoy good health. It is humbling and illuminating to catch the profound meaning of the apostle Paul's statement to Timothy: "If we believe not, yet He abideth faithful: He cannot deny Himself" (2 Timothy 2:13). All man's unfaithfulness, all man's sins,

> . . . alters God no more
> Than our dimmed eyes can quench the stars in heaven.

There is no element of the vindictive in our great and good God.

JUNE 27

Blessings That Lead to Repentance

Or do you show contempt for the riches of his kindness, tolerance and patience, not realizing that God's kindness leads you toward repentance? *(Romans 2:4).*

One of the great marks that the blessings of God are being rightly used is that they lead us to repentance. ". . . not knowing that the goodness of God leadeth thee to repentance?" Repentance in the New Testament sense means just the difference between a sanctified and an unsanctified soul. The only repentant man in the New Testament sense is the holy man, one who is rightly related to God by the Atonement of Jesus and has become a written epistle, "known and read of all men." How many of us have allowed the goodness of God to lead us to repentance? Or are we so enjoying the blessings of God, like the beasts of the field, taking them as our due and not seeing behind them the great loving hand of God, Whose heart is overflowing in tremendous love?

Glorious Uncertainty, But Sure of God

> That is why I am suffering as I am. Yet I am not
> ashamed, because I know whom I have believed, and
> am convinced that he is able to guard what I have
> entrusted to him for that day *(2 Timothy 1:12).*

I n the realm of belief, whenever I become certain of
my creeds, I kill the life of God in my soul, because I
cease to believe in God and believe in my belief instead. All
through the Bible the realm of the uncertain is the realm of
joy and delight; the certainty of belief brings distress.
Certainty of God means uncertainty in life; while certainty
in belief makes us uncertain of God. Certainty is the mark
of the common-sense life; gracious uncertainty is the mark
of the spiritual life, and they must both go together.
Mathematics is the rule of reason and common sense, but
faith and hope is the rule of the spiritual. "It is not yet made
manifest what we shall be"—we are gloriously uncertain of
the next step, but we are certain of God. Immediately we
abandon to God and do the duty that lies nearest, He packs
our lives with surprises all the time.

The Blood of Christ, the Blood of God

> Guard yourselves and all the flock of which the Holy
> Spirit has made you overseers. Be shepherds of the
> church of God, which he bought with his own blood
> *(Acts 20:28).*

I t was not the blood of a martyr, not the blood of goats and calves, that was shed, but "the blood of Christ." The very life of God was shed for the world—"the church of God which He purchased with His own blood." All the perfections of the essential nature of God were in that blood; all the holiest attainments of man were in that blood. The death of Jesus reaches away down underneath the deepest sin human nature ever committed. This aspect of the death of Jesus takes us into a spiritual domain beyond the threshold of the thinking of the majority of us.

JUNE 30 _____

No Answer: But Vision

"My ears had heard of you but now my eyes have seen you. Therefore I despise myself and repent in dust and ashes" *(Job 42:5–6).*

N ow mine eyes seeth Thee, and I abhor my words," i.e., "I abhor the things I was certain of, I abhor myself for being so obstinately certain that I knew; but now I see." In looking at Job's circumstances the curious thing is, he asks conundrum after conundrum, and instead of their being solved, the providence of God hurls more problems at him, till at last Job says, "Now I see." He did not perceive anything in the logical line; he simply found that the interpretation lay with God. Job discerned that truth is never gained by intellect, but by moral conscientiousness. Truth is always a vision that arises in the basis of the moral nature, never in the intellect. Immediately we are rightly related to God in moral relationships, instantly we perceive.

The Secret of True Unity

For we were all baptized by one Spirit into one body—
whether Jews or Greeks, slave or free—and we were all
given the one Spirit to drink *(1 Corinthians 12:13).*

F or by one Spirit are we all baptized into one body.''
The baptism with the Holy Ghost is not only a
personal experience; it is an experience which makes
individual Christians one in the Lord. The only way saints
can meet together as one is through the baptism of the Holy
Ghost, not through external organizations. The end of all
divisions in work for God is when He changes fever into
white-hearted fervour. Oh, the foolish fever there is these
days! Organizing this, organizing that; a fever of intense
activity for God. What is wanted is the baptism with the
Holy Ghost which will mean Our Lord's prayer in John 17
is answered—"that they all may be one; as Thou, Father,
are in Me, and I in Thee, that they also may be one in us"
(v. 21).

Submission to Human Institutions

Submit yourselves for the Lord's sake to every authority
instituted among men: whether to the king, as the
supreme authority, or to governors, who are sent by him
to punish those who do wrong and to commend those
who do right *(1 Peter 2:13–14).*

P eter's statements in these verses are remarkable, and
they are statements the modern Christian does not

like. He is outlining what is to be the conduct of saints in relation to the moral institutions based on the government of man by man. No matter, he says, what may be the condition of the community to which you belong, behave yourself as a saint in it. Many people are righteous as individuals, but they ignore the need to be righteous in connection with human institutions. Paul continually dealt with insubordination in spiritual people. Degeneration in the Christian life comes in because of this refusal to recognize the insistence God places on obedience to human institutions. Take the institution of home life. Home is God's institution, and He says, "Honour thy father and thy mother." Are we fulfilling our duty to our parents as laid down in God's Book?

JULY 3 _____

After Experience, Knowledge

Do you not know that your body is a temple of the Holy Spirit, who is in you, whom you have received from God? You are not your own *(1 Corinthians 6:19)*.

I have to see that I instruct myself regarding these revelations which are only interpreted to me by the Holy Ghost, never by my natural wisdom. There are some saints who are ideally actual, i.e., instructed as well as sanctified, and living in unsullied communion with God, and there are others who are like Ephraim, "a cake not turned." Once let it dawn on your mind that your body is the temple of the Holy Ghost and instantly the impossible becomes possible; the things you used to pray about, you no longer pray about, but *do*. As in the natural world, so in the spiritual, knowledge is power. All we need to *experience* is that we have "passed out of death into life": what we need to *know* takes all Time and Eternity. "And this is life eternal, that they might know Thee the only true God. . . ." (John 17:3). Begin to know Him now.

True Freedom, Not Independence

"Everything is permissible for me"—but not everything is beneficial. "Everything is permissible for me"—but I will not be mastered by anything" *(1 Corinthians 6:12).*

We call liberty allowing the other fellow to please himself to the same extent as we please ourselves. True liberty is the ability earned by practice to do the right thing. There is no such thing as a gift of freedom; freedom must be earned. The counterfeit of freedom is independence. When the Spirit of God deals with sin, it is independence that He touches; that is why the preaching of the Gospel awakens resentment as well as craving. Independence must be blasted right out of a Christian; there must be only liberty, which is a very different thing. Spiritually, liberty means the ability to fulfill the law of God, and it establishes the rights of other people.

All Things Together for Good

And we know that in all things God works for the good of those who love him, who have been called according to his purpose *(Romans 8:28).*

The marvelous thing about the life of God in us is that there is no reaction of exhaustion; it is a continual pouring in all the time. If we work from our own source of energy in a very short time we become artificial, played out, but if we work from the real source of energy, everything that transpires produces "smeddum," a good old Scotch word meaning grit, courage, pluck. Some of us say "I have tried to do all I can for my Church, or my Sunday School class, but it has all failed and I'm going to give it up." That is enervation, i.e., vitality ebbing away because of stagnation somewhere in the vital organs. As long as we whine at circumstances we shall experience the extraordinary trick of providence which keeps us in those circumstances until we learn our lesson. If your circumstances are dark blue just now, remember the time when they were bright pink. It is not the dark blue circumstances that work for our good or the bright pink ones, it is the "togetherness" that does it.

JULY 6 _____

Intercessory Introspection

Search me, O God, and know my heart; test me and know my anxious thoughts. See if there is any offensive way in me, and lead me in the way everlasting *(Psalm 139:23–24)*.

It is a marvelous moment in a man's life when he knows he is explored by God. The tendency in us which makes us want to examine ourselves and know the springs of our thoughts and motives takes the form of prayer, "Search me, O God." The Psalmist speaks of God as the Creator Who knows the vast universe outside, and of

His omnipresence, but he does not end there; he asks this great God to explore him. There is something infinitely more mysterious to the Psalmist than the great universe outside, and that is the mystery of his own heart. There are mountain peaks in my soul, he implies, that I cannot climb; there are ocean depths I cannot fathom; there are possibilities in my heart that terrify me; therefore, O God, search me out. That is intercessory introspection.

JULY 7 _____

His Yoke Beneath the Cross

"Come to me, all you who are weary and burdened, and I will give you rest. Take my yoke upon you and learn from me, for I am gentle and humble in heart and you will find rest for your souls" *(Matthew 11:28–29)*.

The only place we shall find rest is in the direct education by Jesus in His Cross. A new delight springs up in any saint who suffers the yoke of Christ. Beware of dissipating that yoke and making it mean the yoke of a martyr. It is the yoke of a person who owes all he has to the Cross of Christ. Paul wore the yoke when he said, "For I determined not to know anything among you, save Jesus Christ, and Him crucified." "Take My yoke upon you"—it is the one yoke men will not wear.

Have I taken the yoke of Christ upon me, and am I walking in the innocent light that comes only from the Spirit of God through the Atonement?

146

Spiritual Gluttony

This is the man who will dwell on the heights, whose refuge will be the mountain fortress. His bread will be supplied, and water will not fail him *(Isaiah 33:16)*.

"The days are coming," declares the Sovereign LORD,"when I will send a famine through the land—not a famine of food or a thirst for water, but a famine of hearing the words of the LORD." *(Amos 8:11)*.

T wo things the Bible states are sure for men if they obey God—bread and water (see Isaiah 33:16); that is all God has promised us. Look over the history of civilizations and you will find every disaster has come by taking more. A spiritual application may be made along this line—"a famine of hearing the words of the Lord" strikes every soul that has departed from the living God and dwelt by pleasant spiritual experiences—God's word dead to you, no inspiration about it; prayer dead, spiritual communion dead, you wait and long and pray and nothing happens, everything languishing and dying. You will find if sin has not been the cause, there has been a selfish glutting of your soul on experiences instead of going on to know God Who gave you the experiences. We refuse to eat the old corn of the land, we prefer manna—that God should always do some exceptional thing for us.

An Eternal Principle

"For whoever wants to save his life will lose it, but whoever loses his life for me will find it" *(Matthew 16:25)*.

We must bear in mind that Our Lord in His teaching reveals unalterable and eternal principles. In this Scripture, Jesus says that the eternal principle of human life is that something must be sacrificed; if we won't sacrifice the natural life, we do the spiritual. Our Lord is not speaking of a punishment to be meted out; he is revealing what is God's eternal principle at the back of human life. We may rage and fret, as men have done, against God's just principles, or we may submit and accept and go on; but Jesus reveals that these principles are as unalterable as God Himself.

My Attitude to Another's Sin

Although our sins testify against us, O Lord, do something for the sake of your name. For our backsliding is great; we have sinned against you *(Jeremiah 14:7)*.

If anyone sees his brother commit a sin that does not lead to death, he should pray and God will give him life. I refer to those whose sin does not lead to death. I am not saying he should pray about that (1 John 5:16).

We have sinned against Thee." There is a difference between a moralist's and a Christian's condemnation of sin. A spiritual Christian always feels the unmitigated horror of the sin of another. A moralist never does; to him it is an occasion to "lambast" something that is wrong. A Christian knows the possibilities of every sin ever committed are in him but for the grace of God. The condemnation of sin before we are saved is bitter, intense, and proud. After we are saved, the sins of others come upon us with the twofold weight of the possibility of doing the like ourselves, and the possibility of vicarious intercession.

"Why shouldest Thou be . . . as a mighty man that cannot save?" (Jeremiah 14:9). Why does God not speak? This is not atheism, but the agony of a human heart getting into the secret of the Cross.

JULY 11 _____

Watching and Waiting

> I will stand at my watch and station myself on the ramparts; I will look to see what he will say to me, and what answer I am to give to this complaint (Habakkuk 2:1).

Watch for God's answers to your prayers, and not only watch but wait. When God calls upon you to pray, when He gives you the vision, when He gives you an understanding of what He is going to do through you in your Sunday school class, in your Church or home—watch. How many of us have had to learn by God's reproof, by God's chastisement, the blunder of conferring with flesh and blood. Are you discouraged where you are, worker? Then get upon this tower with God, and watch, and wait. The meaning of waiting in both Old and New Testament is "standing under," actively enduring. It is not standing with folded arms doing nothing; it is not saying.

149

"In God's good time it will come to pass"—that often means, "In my abominably lazy time I let God work." Waiting means standing under, in active strength, enduring till the answer comes.

JULY 12

Our Loyalty to His Royalty

"You are a king, then!" said Pilate. Jesus answered, "You are right in saying I am a king. In fact, for this reason I was born, and for this I came into the world, to testify to the truth. Everyone on the side of truth listens to me" *(John 18:37).*

J esus Christ is not only Saviour, He is King, and He has the right to exact anything and everything from us at His own discretion. We talk about the joys and comforts of salvation; Jesus Christ talks about taking up the cross and following Him. Whenever Our Lord talks about discipleship He prefaces it with an "'If'"—"you need not unless you like." It is always easier in certain crises to be "Demas" than a devoted disciple. Very few of us know anything about loyalty to Jesus Christ. "For My sake"—that is what makes the iron saint. We look upon Jesus Christ as the best Example of the Christian life; we do not conceive of Him as Almighty God Incarnate, with all power in heaven and on earth. We deal with Him as if He were one of ourselves; we do not take off the shoes from our feet when He speaks. Jesus Christ is Saviour, and He saves us into His own absolute and holy lordship.

150

The Motive Behind Our Righteousness

Dear children, do not let anyone lead you astray. He who does what is right is righteous, just as he is righteous *(1 John 3:7)*.

T here are different kinds of intention, e.g., outer and inner; immediate and remote; direct and indirect. The righteous man is the one whose inner intention is clearly revealed in his outer intention; there is no duplicity, no internal hypocrisy. A man's outer intention is easily discernible by other people; his inner intention needs to be continually examined. The marvel of the grace of God is that it can alter the mainspring of our make-up; then when that is altered we must foster in ourselves those intentions which spring from the Spirit of Jesus and make our nervous system carry them out. The Holy Spirit will bring us to the practical test; it is not that I *say* I am righteous, but that I prove I am in my deeds.

Bondslaves of Jesus

As a result, it has become clear throughout the whole palace guard and to everyone else that I am in chains for Christ *(Philippians 1:13)*.

T he passion of Christianity is that I deliberately sign away my own rights and become a bondslave of Jesus Christ. Any fool can insist on his rights, and any devil will see that he gets them; but the Sermon on the Mount means that the only right the saint will insist on is the right to give up his rights. That is the New Testament idea of sanctification, and that is why so few get anywhere near the baptism with the Holy Ghost. "I want to be baptized with the Holy Ghost so that I may be of use"—then it is all up.

JULY 15 _____

Mastered by the Master

> "You call me 'Teacher' and 'Lord,' and rightly so, for that is what I am. Now that I, your Lord and Teacher, have washed your feet, you also should wash one another's feet. I have set you an example that you should do as I have done for you. I tell you the truth, no servant is greater than his master, nor is a messenger greater than the one who sent him. Now that you know these things, you will be blessed if you do them" *(John 13:13–17).*

Whenever a man is mastered by Jesus Christ you have a man "with breast and back as either should be," no whimperer, no sentimentalist, no pietist, but a man of God. That can only be produced by the mastership of Jesus Christ. The curious thing about Our Lord is that He never insists on our obedience. When we begin to usurp authority and say, "You must" and "you shall" it is a sure sign that we are out of touch with the supreme Authority. If you are in a position of authority and people are not obeying you, the greatest heart-searching you can have is the realization that the blame does not lie with them, but with you; there is a leakage going on spiritually. Get right with God yourself, and every other one will get in touch with God through you.

Self Truly Realized in Love to God

" 'Love the Lord your God with all your heart and with all your soul and with all your mind and with all your strength.' The second is this: 'Love your neighbor as yourself.' There is no commandment greater than these" *(Mark 12:30–31).*

Man was created to be the friend and lover of God and for no other end, and until he realizes this he will go through turmoil and upset. Human nature must rise to its own Source, the bosom of God, and Jesus Christ by His Redemption brings it back there. God is the only One who has the right to myself and when I love Him with all my heart and soul and mind and strength, self in its essence is realized. All the teaching of Jesus is woven around self; I have a moral self-love to preserve for God. Not, "Oh, I'm of no account, a worm"; that would spell self-less-ness. "I hold not my life of any account, as dear unto myself," says Paul, "so that I may accomplish my course, and the ministry which I received from the Lord Jesus, to testify the gospel of the grace of God." That is, he refused to use himself for any other interest but God's, and for that which glorified God.

What Is Perfect Love?

Whoever does not love does not know God, because God is love. This is how God showed his love among us: He sent his one and only Son into the world that we might live through him. This is love: not that we loved

God, but that he loved us and sent his Son as an atoning sacrifice for our sins. Dear friends, since God so loved us, we also ought to love one another. No one has ever seen God; but if we love each other, God lives in us and his love is made complete in us *(1 John 4:8–12)*.

B ut let the lowliest soul whose influence apparently amounts to nothing get rightly related to God, and out of him will flow rivers of living water which he does not see, but one day we shall find that it is those lives which have been spreading the lasting benediction. "Love is of God"; it never came from the devil and never can go to the devil. When I am rightly related to God, the more I love the more blessing does He pour out on other lives. The reward of love is the capacity to pour out more love all the time, "hoping for nothing again." That is the essential nature of perfect love.

The true import of love is the surrender of myself, I go out of myself in order to live in and for God. To be indwelt by the Spirit of Jesus means I am willing to quit my own abode from the self-interested standpoint and live only in and for God.

JULY 18 _____

Self-Sacrifice or Obedience

But Samuel replied: "Does the LORD delight in burnt offerings and sacrifices as much as in obeying the voice of the LORD? To obey is better than sacrifice, and to heed is better than the fat of rams" *(1 Samuel 15:22)*.

Therefore, when Christ came into the world, he said: "Sacrifice and offering you did not desire, but a body you prepared for me; with burnt offerings and sin

154

offerings you were not pleased. Then I said, 'Here I am—it is written about me in the scroll—I have come to do your will, O God' " *(Hebrews 10:5–7).*

B ehold, to obey is better than sacrifice." Self-sacrifice may be simply a disease of the nerves, a morbid self-consciousness which is the obverse of intense selfishness. Our Lord never confounds selfishness and self. Whenever I make self-sacrifice the aim and end of my life, I become a traitor to Jesus; instead of placing Him as my Lodestar I place Him as an example, One who helps me to sacrifice myself. I am not saved to sacrifice; I am saved to fulfill my destiny in Christ. It is much easier to sacrifice myself, to efface myself, than to do God's will in His way.

JULY 19 _____

Perfectly Fit, But . . .

All of us who are mature should take such a view of things. And if on some point you think differently, that too God will make clear to you *(Philippians 3:15).*

L et us therefore as many as be perfect . . ."—Paul implies, "Now remember though you have been perfectly adjusted to God through the Redemption, you have attained to nothing yet." The idea is that of a marathon runner, practicing and practising until he is perfectly fit; when he is perfectly fit, he hasn't begun his race; he is only perfectly fit to begin. By regeneration we are put into perfect relation with God; then it is the same human nature, working on the same lines, but with a different mainspring. "Not that I have already obtained, or am already made perfect": that is the perfection of

155

consummation, "I haven't got there yet," says Paul; "but I press on if so be that I may apprehend that for which also I was apprehended by Christ Jesus."

_____

False Shepherds and True

"Son of Man, prophesy against the shepherds of Israel; prophesy and say to them: 'This is what the Sovereign LORD says: Woe to the shepherds of Israel who only take care of themselves! Should not shepherds take care of the flock? You eat the curds, clothe yourselves with the wool and slaughter the choice animals, but you do not take care of the flock. You have not strengthened the weak or healed the sick or bound up the injured. You have not brought back the strays or searched for the lost. You have ruled them harshly and brutally. So they were scattered because there was no shepherd, and when they were scattered they became food for all the wild animals. My sheep wandered over all the mountains and on every high hill. They were scattered over the whole earth, and no one searched or looked for them. "Therefore, you shepherds, hear the word of the LORD: As surely as I live, declares the Sovereign LORD because my flock lacks a shepherd and so has been plundered and has become food for all the wild animals, and because my shepherds did not search for my flock but cared for themselves rather than for my flock . . . I am against the shepherds and will hold them accountable for my flock" *(Ezekiel 34:2–8, 10).*

Again Jesus said, "Simon son of John, do you truly love me?" He answered, "Yes, Lord, You know that I love you." Jesus said, "Take care of my sheep" *(John 21:16)*.

S hould not the shepherds feed the sheep?" In the New Testament the terms *shepherd* and *sheep* are applied not to kings and nations, but to the disciples of Jesus. When Our Lord commissioned Peter He did not tell him to go and save souls, but— "Feed My sheep; tend My lambs; guard My flock." We have to be careful lest we rebel against the commission to disciple men to Jesus and become energetic proselytizers to our own way of thinking— "but the shepherds fed themselves, and fed not My sheep;" (v. 8). When we stand before God will He say, "You have not been a shepherd of My sheep, you have fed them for your own interest, exploited them for your own creed"? When a soul gets within sight of Jesus Christ, leave him alone.

JULY 21 _____

Fulfilling the Law Through Christ

Be found in him, not having a righteousness of my own that comes from the law, but that which is through faith in Christ—the righteousness that comes from God and is by faith *(Philippians 3:9)*.

S aul of Tarsus did easily what other Pharisees did, but his conscience would not allow him to be a hypocrite easily. His ardent nature tried to make his inner life come up to the standard of the law, and the tragedy of his failure is expressed in Romans 7. No one was ever so introspective, so painfully conscious of his weakness and inability to keep the law; consequently when he says, "Christ is the end of the law unto righteousness," he is making the most intensely practical statement that could be made. He is stating the fact that Christ had planted in him as a sheer gift of God's grace the life which enabled him now easily to fulfill all the law of God—"not having a righteousness of mine own, . . . but that which is through faith in Christ." *"Imputed"* with Paul always means *"imparted."*

JULY 22 _____

The Subtle Sin of Pride

> "Son of man, say to the ruler of Tyre, 'This is what the Sovereign LORD says: "In the pride of your heart you say, I am a god; I sit on the throne of a god in the heart of the seas." But you are a man and not a god, though you think you are as wise as a god' " *(Ezekiel 28:2).*

P ride in its most estimable as well as its most debased form is self-deification; it is not a yielding to temptation from without, but a distinct alteration of relationships within. Watch where you are not willing to give up your self-confident obstinacy in little things, and you will know how much pride there is in your heart, how much you will set your moral teeth against God's providential order—"I won't yield"; "I won't for a second allow anyone to usurp my rights." To that life will come the revelation of God as an enemy. If we have had detected in us any lurking of pride, when are we going to break from it? We will have to break some day, why not now?

Are We Going on to Apprehend?

Not that I have already obtained all this, or have already been made perfect, but I press on to take hold of that for which Christ Jesus took hold of me *(Philippians 3:12)*.

P aul reverted to one thing only—"When it was the good pleasure of God, . . . to reveal His Son to me"; then he never bothered about himself any more. We try to lose ourselves and efface ourselves by an effort; Paul did not efface himself by an effort; his interest in himself simply died right out when he became identified with Christ and Him crucified. We are all more or less keenly interested in the work of grace in our souls, but the reason we don't go on to "apprehend that for which we were apprehended by Christ" is that there are whole tracts of our nature which have never been fused by the fire of God into one central purpose. How long it takes till all our powers are at one depends on one thing only, viz., obedience.

The Strangeness of His "Faithfulness"

Then Jesus told his disciples a parable to show them that they should always pray and not give up. He said: "In a certain town there was a judge who neither feared God nor cared about men. And there was a widow in that town who kept coming to him with the plea, 'Grant me justice against my adversary.' For some time he refused. But finally he said to himself, 'Even though I don't fear God or care about men, yet because this widow keeps bothering me, I will see that she gets justice, so that she won't eventually wear me out with her coming!' " And the Lord said, "Listen to what the unjust judge says. And will not God bring about justice for his chosen ones, who cry out to him day and night? Will he keep putting them off? I tell you, he will see that they get justice, and quickly. However, when the Son of Man comes, will he find faith on the earth?" *(Luke 18:1–8).*

Human life is not made up of right and wrong, but of things which are not quite clear—"I do not know what God would have me do in this matter." Stand off in faith that what Jesus said is true—*everyone that asks receives,* and in the meantime do the duty that lies nearest, waiting and watching. If the friendship of God is shrouded and it looks as if He is not going to do anything, then remain dumb. The real problems are very heavy. Instead of God being a Father loving and kind, it looks at times as if He were totally indifferent. Remember, God has bigger issues at stake on the ground of His Redemption than the particular setting in which we ask. In the meantime we do not know what God is doing, but we are certain that what Jesus says is true. "If ye then, being evil, know how to give good gifts unto your children, how much more shall your Heavenly Father give the Holy Spirit to them that ask Him?" When we are the possessors of the Holy Spirit, we shall justify God all through.

JULY 25 _____

Blessing Through the Word

"As the rain and the snow come down from heaven, and do not return to it without watering the earth and making it bud and flourish, so that it yields seed for the sower and bread for the eater, so is my word that goes out from my mouth: It will not return to me empty, but will accomplish what I desire and achieve the purpose for which I sent it" *(Isaiah 55:10–11).*

G od's Word is as a seed. The "seed-thought" idea is one that preachers and evangelists need to remember. We imagine we have to plough the field, sow the seed, reap the grain, bind it into sheaves, put it through the threshing machine, make the bread—all in one discourse. "For herein is the saying true, One soweth, and another reapeth," said our Lord. Let each one be true to the calling given him by God. The truth is we don't believe God can do His work without us. We are so anxious about the Word, so anxious about the people who have accepted the Word; we need not be, if we have preached what is a Word of God, it is not our business to apply it; the Holy Spirit will apply it.

JULY 26 _____

The Living Word in the Written Word

Above all, you must understand that no prophecy of Scripture came about by the prophet's own interpretation *(2 Peter 1:20).*

J ust as Jesus Christ is the final revelation of God, so the Bible is the final revelation interpreting Him. Our Lord Jesus Christ (The Word of God) and the Bible (the accompanying revelation) stand or fall together; they can never be separated without fatal results. The words of the Bible apart from being interpreted by the Word of God, are worse than lifeless, they kill (2 Cor. 3:6). But when a soul is

161

born from above and lifted to the atmosphere of the domain where our Lord lives, the Bible becomes its native air; its words become the storehouse of omnipotence, its commands and prophecies become alive; its limitless horizons brace the heart and mind to a new consciousness; its comforts in Psalms and prayers and exhortations delight the whole man. And better than all, the Lord Jesus Christ becomes the altogether Lovely One; it is in His light that we see light, it is in Him that we become new creatures. He who is the Word of God unfolds to us the revelation of God until we say in sacred rapture, "I hold in my hands the Thought of God."

JULY 27

The Shadow of His Fatherhood

"Which of you fathers, if your son asks for a fish, will give him a snake instead? Or if he asks for an egg, will give him a scorpion?" *(Luke 11:12)*.

J esus says there are times when our Heavenly Father will appear as if He were a most unnatural father, callous and indifferent—I asked for bread and He gave me a stone, and there is a shadow on His Fatherhood. But remember, says Jesus, I have told you—*everyone that asks receives*. When we get into spiritual confusion the usual way out is to say we have made a blunder, and we go back instead of forward. "I don't know what to do; I am up against a stone wall." Will you "hang in" to what Jesus said? If there is a shadow on the face of the Fatherhood of God just now, remain confident that ultimately He will give His clear issue as Jesus said. It is not a question of black or white, of right or wrong; of being in communion or out of communion; but a question of God taking us by a way which in the meantime we do not understand.

Faith and Prayer in the Details

Hezekiah received the letter from the messengers and read it. Then he went up to the temple of the Lord and spread it out before the Lord *(Isaiah 37:14).*

These have come so that your faith—of greater worth than gold, which perishes even though refined by fire—may be proved genuine and may result in praise, glory and honor when Jesus Christ is revealed *(1 Peter 1:7).*

F aith is the trend of the life all through, and everything that is not "hid with Christ in God" is against it. The trial of faith always comes in such a way that it is a perplexity to know what to do. You get advice that sounds wise, it has your welfare in view, everything seems right, and yet there is the feeling that there is an error at the heart of it.

"And Hezekiah received the letter from the hand of the messengers, and read it: and Hezekiah went up unto the house of the Lord, and spread it before the Lord" (v. 14). If any letter is not important enough to be "spread before the Lord," it is too small to annoy you. If I have not prayed about things so ridiculously small that I almost blush to mention them, I have not learned the first lesson in prayer.

Our Anguish in God's Fire

"Am I the sea, or the monster of the deep, that you put
me under guard? When I think my bed will comfort me
and my couch will ease my complaint, even then you
frighten me with dreams and terrify me with visions, so
that I prefer strangling and death, rather than this body of
mine. I despise my life; I would not live forever. Let me
alone; my days have no meaning. What is man that you
make so much of him, that you give him so much
attention, that you examine him every morning and test
him every moment?" *(Job 7:12–18).*

J ob gives utterance to a mood which is not foreign to
us when he says, "Am I a sea, or a whale, that Thou
settest a watch over me?" In certain moods of anguish the
human heart says to God, "I wish You would let me alone;
why should I be used for things which have no appeal to
me?" In the Christian life we are not being used for our
own designs at all, but for the fulfillment of the prayer of
Jesus Christ. He has prayed that we might be "one with
Him as He is one with the Father," consequently God is
concerned only about that one thing, and He never says
"By your leave." Whether we like it or not, God will burn
us in His fire until we are as pure as He is, and it is during
the process that we cry, as Job did, "I wish You would
leave me alone." God is the only Being who can afford to
be misunderstood; we cannot, Job could not, but God can.

The Supplanter Becomes a Warrior

The man asked him, "What is your name?" "Jacob," he
answered *(Genesis 32:27)*.

T he confession has to be made—"That is my name—
  sneak, supplanter"; there is no palliation. This is full
and profound and agonizing repentance. Jacob had to get
to the place where he willingly confesses before God the
whole guilt of his usurping the birthright. "And he said,
'Thy name shall be called no more Jacob, but Israel: for
thou hast striven with God and with men, and hast
prevailed.' " The warrior of God is not the man of muscle
and a strong jaw, but the man of unutterable weakness; the
man who knows he has not any power instantly becomes a
warrior of God. Jacob is no longer strong in himself, he is
strong only in the Lord; his life is no longer marked by his
own striving but by reliance on God. You cannot imitate
reliance on God.

The Renewal of the Mind

Do not conform any longer to the pattern of this world,
but be transformed by the renewing of your mind. Then
you will be able to test and approve what God's will is—
his good, pleasing and perfect will *(Romans 12:2)*.

A lways remember that Jesus Christ's statements force
  an issue of will and conscience first, and only as we
obey is there the understanding with the mind (see John
7:17). The challenge to the will comes in the matter of

study, as long as you remain in the "stodge" state there is no mental progress—"I am overwhelmed by the tremendous amount there is to know and it's no use my going on." If you will forge through that stage you will suddenly turn a corner where everything that was difficult and perplexing becomes as clear as a lightening flash, but it all depends on whether you will forge ahead. When people say, "Preach us the simple Gospel," what they mean is, "Preach us the thing we have always heard, the thing that keeps us sound asleep; we don't want to see things differently"; then the sooner the Spirit of God sends a thrust through their stagnant minds the better. Continual renewal of mind is the only healthy state for a Christian. Beware of the ban of finality about your present views.

AUGUST 1 _____

The Only Safe Place

What answer shall be given to the envoys of that nation? "The LORD has established Zion, and in her his afflicted people will find refuge" *(Isaiah 14:32)*.

T he Lord hath founded Zion, and in her shall the afflicted of His people take refuge" (cf. 14:32). Just as Zion is spoken of as the central place of safety for the nations, so the only safe place for the saint, and it is as safe as God Himself, is the secret place of the Most High, abiding under the shadow of the Almighty (cf. Psalm 125:1–2). The same great majestic note is brought out in Psalm 46—"Therefore will not we fear, though . . ." It is the grand position got from the great God.

Undisturbed in Disturbance

You have been a refuge for the poor, a refuge for the
needy in his distress, a shelter from the storm and a
shade from the heat: For the breath of the ruthless is like
a storm driving against a wall and like the heat of the
desert. You silence the uproar of foreigners; as heat is
reduced by the shadow of a cloud, so the song of the
ruthless is stilled *(Isaiah 25:4–5).*

T he great thing about faith in God is that it keeps a
man undisturbed in the midst of disturbance. Every
now and again God lets loose the hounds of hell all around
you, and if you are His child, indwelt by His Spirit, you will
experience the truth that Isaiah proclaims, viz., that all the
forces outside you are futile because they are less powerful
than the indwelling of God (see 1 John 4:4). No matter
what may be the changing of forceful interests all around,
the work of God's grace stands true in His servants.

The Only Thing That Remains

"But God said to him, 'You fool! This very night your life
will be demanded from you. Then who will get what you
have prepared for yourself?' " *(Luke 12:20).*

W e estimate by what a man possesses; God's only
concern is what a man *is.* There is only one thing that
will endure and that is personality; no possessions, no
pretence, nothing in the way of what men call greatness will
last. All the rest is trappings, in their right place, great and

167

good trappings, but Satan wants to keep our minds on them. Holiness in character is the only thing that will remain. Some of us will have a spiritual character so microscopic that it will take the archangels to find it!

AUGUST 4 _____

Carefully Careless

"Therefore I tell you, do not worry about your life, what you will eat or drink; or about your body, what you will wear. Is not life more important than food, and the body more important than clothes? Look at the birds of the air; they do not sow or reap or store away in barns, and yet your heavenly Father feeds them. Are you not much more valuable than they? Who of you by worrying can add a single hour to his life?" *(Matthew 6:25–27).*

T he most seriously minded Christian is the one who has just become a Christian; the mature saint is just like a young child, absolutely simple and joyful and gay. Read the Sermon on the Mount—"Take no thought," [i.e., no care] "for your life." The word *care* has within it the idea of something that buffets. The Christianity of Jesus Christ refuses to be careworn. Our Lord is indicating that we have to be carefully careless about everything saving our relationship to Him.

AUGUST 5 _____

The Road Back to Yesterday

"I will repay you for the years the locusts have eaten— the great locust and the young locust, the other locusts and the locust swarm—my great army that I sent among you" *(Joel 2:25).*

F orgiveness does not mean merely that I am saved from sin and made right for heaven; forgiveness means that I am forgiven into a recreated relationship to God.

Do I believe that God can deal with my "yesterday," and make it as though it had never been? I either do not believe he can, or I do not want Him to. Forgiveness, which is so easy for us to accept, cost God the agony of Calvary. When Jesus Christ says "Sin no more," He conveys the power that enables a man not to sin any more, and that power comes by right of what He did on the Cross.

AUGUST 6 _____

The "Profane Man"

See that no one is sexually immoral, or is godless like Esau, who for a single meal sold his inheritance rights as the oldest son *(Hebrews 12:16).*

I loved Jacob"—God loves the man who needs Him. Esau was satisfied with what he was; Jacob wanted more than he was. Esau never saw visions, or wrestled with angels, although God was as near to him as He was to Jacob. He refused to sacrifice anything to the spiritual. Esau could never think of anything but the present; he was willing to sell the promise of the future for a mess of pottage, and thereby he wronged himself more than Jacob did.

The Wonder of Bethel

When Jacob awoke from his sleep, he thought, "Surely the LORD is in this place, and I was not aware of it." He was afraid and said, "How awesome is this place! This is none other than the house of God; this is the gate of heaven" *(Genesis 28:16–17).*

T his place" means just where it is not within the bounds of imagination to infer that God would be. "And he called the name of that place Beth-el . . ." (v. 19) "because there God was revealed unto him" (35:7). "Every house of God is a gate of heaven where the impossible and the miraculous become the natural breath." There is always an amazed surprise when we find what God brings with Him when He comes; He brings everything! (cf. John 14:23).

Receiving His Peace

"Peace I leave with you; my peace I give you. I do not give to you as the world gives. Do not let your hearts be troubled and do not be afraid" *(John 14:27).*

T he disciples, like many to-day, were not in a state to provide their own inner peace. There are times when inner peace is based on ignorance; but when we awake to the troubles of life, which more than ever before surge and heave in threatening billows, inner peace is impossible unless it is received from our Lord. When our Lord spoke peace, He made peace. His words are ever "spirit and life." Have you ever received what He spoke?

AUGUST 9 _____

The God of Jacob

The LORD Almighty is with us; the God of Jacob is our fortress *(Psalm 46:11).*

When we come to consider it, the phrase "the God of Jacob" is the greatest possible inspiration; it has in it the whole meaning of the Gospel of Jesus Christ, who said He came not to call the righteous but sinners. Had we been left with such phrases as "the God of Joseph," or "the God of Daniel," it would have spelt hopeless despair for most of us; but "the God of Jacob" means—"God is *my* God," the God of the sneak, not only of the noble characters. From the sneak to entire sanctification is the miracle of the grace of God.

AUGUST 10 _____

Telling God What He Knows

Hezekiah received the letter from the messengers and read it. Then he went up to the temple of the LORD and spread it out before the LORD. And Hezekiah prayed to the LORD: "O LORD Almighty, God of Israel, enthroned between the cherubim, you alone are God over all the kingdoms of the earth. You have made heaven and earth. Give ear, O LORD, and hear; open your eyes, O LORD and see; listen to all the words Sennacherib has sent to insult the living God. "It is true, O LORD, that the

Assyrian kings have laid waste all these peoples and their lands. They have thrown their gods into the fire and destroyed them, for they were not gods but only wood and stone, fashioned by human hands. Now, O LORD,our God, deliver us from his hand, so that all kingdoms on earth may know that you alone, O LORD,are God." *(Isaiah 37:14–20)*.

To the rationalist it is ridiculous to pray to God about everything; behind the ridicule is the devil to keep us from knowing the road when the crisis comes. Hezekiah knew the road. In his prayer (vv. 16–20) Hezekiah tells God what he knows God knows already. That is the meaning of prayer—I tell God what I know He knows in order that I may get to know it as He does (cf. Matthew 6:8). It is not true to say that a man learns to pray in calamities, he never does; he calls on God to deliver him, but he does not pray (see Psalm 107:6, 13, 19); a man only learns to pray when there is no calamity.

AUGUST 11 _____

Man's Destiny: Salvation or Damnation?

Then the LORD said to Jacob, "Go back to the land of your fathers and to your relatives, and I will be with you" *(Genesis 31:3)*.

And the Lord said unto Jacob, Return."
No man's destiny is made for him, each man makes his own. Fatalism is the deification of moral cowardice which arises from a refusal to accept the responsibility for choosing either of the two destined ends for the human race—salvation or damnation. The power of individual choice is the secret of human responsibility. I can choose

which line I will go on, but I have no power to alter the destination of that line when once I have taken it—yet I always have the power to get off one line on to the other.

AUGUST 12

The Sense of the Irreparable

He said, "May the day of my birth perish, and the night it was said, 'A boy is born!' " *(Job 3:2–3)*.

I t is a sad thing that Job is facing, and it seems that the only reasonable thing he can do is to mourn the day of his birth. With some people suffering is imaginary, but with Job it has actually happened, and his curse is the real deep conviction of his spirit—"Would to God I had never been born!" The sense of the irreparable is one of the greatest agonies in human life. Adam and Eve entered into the sense of the irreparable when the gates of Paradise clanged behind them. Cain cried out—"My punishment is greater than I can bear." Esau "found no place of repentance, though he sought it diligently with tears." There are things in life which are irreparable; there is no road back to yesterday.

AUGUST 13

Strangers and Sojourners

"I am an alien and a stranger among you. Sell me some property for a burial site here so I can bury my dead" *(Genesis 23:4)*.

173

All these people were still living by faith when they died. They did not receive the things promised; they only saw them and welcomed them from a distance. And they admitted that they were aliens and strangers on earth *(Hebrews 11:13).*

T he phrase Abraham uses, "a stranger and sojourner," is the inner meaning of the term *Hebrew.* Abraham could never say that he was at home in Canaan; he left his home never to find another on earth. The thought of pilgrimage sank deep into the Hebrew mind, and the note of the sojourner is essentially the note of the Christian. Instead of being pilgrims and strangers on the earth, we become citizens of this order of things and entrench ourselves there, and the statements of Jesus have no meaning. The genius of the Spirit of God is to make us pilgrims.

In dealing with the life of Abraham neither faith nor common sense must be our guide, but God Who unites both in the alchemy of personal experience. To be guided by common sense alone is fanatical; both common sense and faith have to be brought into relation to God. The life of faith does not consist of acts of worship or of great self-denial and heroic virtues, but of all the daily conscious acts of our lives.

AUGUST 14 _____

Human Wits Versus Divine Wisdom

So he fled with all he had, and crossing the River, he headed for the hill country of Gilead *(Genesis 31:21).*

J acob, of all the Bible characters, ever remains the best example of the recipient of God's life and power, simply because of the appalling mixture of the good and the bad, the noble and ignoble, in him. His towering nobility is never far to seek in the midst of all his abominations. We have the notion that it is only when we are pure and right and holy that God will appear to us; also we are apt to say that God's blessing is a sign that we are right with Him.

AUGUST 15 _____

After Surrender, What?

"Come to me, all you who are weary and burdened, and I will give you rest" *(Matthew 11:28)*.

Then Jesus said to his disciples, "If anyone would come after me, he must deny himself and take up his cross and follow me" *(Matthew 16:24)*.

H as Jesus Christ saved you by His sovereign grace? Has He given you His rest? If He has not, there is no use praying about it; there is only one thing to do—come to Him and take it. Or has Jesus Christ been trying to get you to surrender yourself to be a disciple of His? He brought you to the point long ago but you balked it again and again. Or is it a question of being united with the death of Jesus until nothing ever appeals to you that did not appeal to Him?

After surrender—what? The whole of the life after surrender is an aspiration, an aspiration after unbroken communion with God.

The Snare of Superstition

Now Rachel had taken the household gods and put them inside her camel's saddle and was sitting on them. Laban searched through everything in the tent but found nothing *(Genesis 31:34).*

A mascot is a talisman of some sort whose presence is supposed to bring good luck. The persistence of the superstitious element is one of the most indelible stains on the character of otherwise good people, and it abounds in our own day. A reawakening of superstition always follows on the heels of gross materialism in either personal or national life. When once the "mascot" tendency is allowed in the temple of the Holy Ghost, spiritual muddle-headedness is sure to result. Beware of excusing spiritual muddle-headedness in yourself; if it is not produced by the "Jacob" reserve, it is produced by the "Rachel" wit, and the only way out of the muddle is to walk in the light as God is in the light.

Christian Love in Action

Love is patient, love is kind. It does not envy, it does not boast, it is not proud. It is not rude, it is not self-seeking, it is not easily angered, it keeps no record of wrongs. Love does not delight in evil but rejoices with the truth. It always protects, always trusts, always hopes, always perseveres *(1 Corinthians 13:4–7).*

L ove is the sovereign preference of my person for another person, and Jesus demands that that other Person be Himself; and the direction of Divine living is that I deliberately identify myself with Jesus Christ's interests in other people. "Love suffereth long, and is kind; love envieth not; love seeketh not its own, is not provoked, taketh not account of evil, beareth all things, believeth all things, hopeth all things, endureth all things. Love never faileth." That is Christian living in actual life. If I have the disposition of a fault-finder, I am a most uncomfortable person to live with, but if the love of God has been shed abroad in my heart, I begin to see extraordinary self-sacrifice under the roughest of exteriors.

AUGUST 18 _____

The Test of Spiritual Education

For this very reason, make every effort to add to your faith goodness; and to goodness, knowledge; and to knowledge, self-control; and to self-control, perseverance; and to perseverance, godliness; and to godliness, brotherly kindness; and to brotherly kindness, love (2 Peter 1:5–7).

A m I getting nobler, better, more helpful, more humble, as I get older? Am I exhibiting the life that men take knowledge of as having been with Jesus, or am I getting more self-assertive, more deliberately determined to have my own way? It is a great thing to tell yourself the truth.

These are some of the lines of spiritual education: learning the dimensions of Divine Love, that the center of that love is holiness; that the direction of Divine living is a

deliberate surrender of our own point of view in order to
learn Jesus Christ's point of view, and seeing that men and
women are nourished in the knowledge of Jesus. The only
way that can be done is by being loyal to Jesus myself.

AUGUST 19 _____

The Cross, Revealing the Love of a Holy God

This is love: not that we loved God, but that he loved us
and sent his Son as an atoning sacrifice for our sins
(1 John 4:10).

I n the Cross we may see the dimensions of Divine
Love. The Cross is not the cross of a man, but the
exhibition of the heart of God. At the back of the wall of the
world stands God with His arms outstretched, and every
man driven there is driven into the arms of God. The Cross
of Jesus is the supreme evidence of the love of God
(Romans 8:35–39). "Who shall separate us from the love
of Christ?" (v. 35).

The Cross of Christ reveals that the blazing center of the
love of God is the holiness of God, not His kindness and
compassion. If the Divine love pretends I am all right when I
am all wrong, then I have a keener sense of justice than the
Almighty. God is a holy God, and the marvel of the
Redemption is that God the Holy One puts into me, the
unholy one, a new disposition, the disposition of His Son.

Not Consecration But Concentration

In the sixth year, in the sixth month on the fifth day, while I was sitting in my house and the elders of Judah were sitting before me, the hand of the Sovereign LORD came upon me there *(Ezekiel 8:1)*.

E zekiel's abstraction is typical of spiritual concentration—shut out from external things for concentration on the purpose of God. The great need for Christians today is occasional fasting from intellectual and religious and social activities in order to give ourselves wholly to the realization of some purpose of God. Acts of consecration and devotional exercises leave us much the same; concentration on God never leaves us the same. This place is for concentration on God and on nothing else.

A Prophet's Portrait of Christ

Who has believed our message and to whom has the arm of the LORD been revealed? He grew up before him like a tender shoot, and like a root out of dry ground. He had no beauty or majesty to attract us to him, nothing in his appearance that we should desire him. He was despised and rejected by men, a man of sorrows, and familiar with suffering. Like one from whom men hide their faces he was despised, and we esteemed him not. Surely he took up our infirmities and carried our sorrows, yet we considered him stricken by God, smitten by him, and afflicted. But he was pierced for our transgressions, he was crushed for our iniquities; the punishment that brought us peace was upon him, and by his wounds we are healed *(Isaiah 53:1–5)*.

I f you want to know the characterization of the Person of Christ you will find it here, sketched by His Father, through the mouth of Isaiah. The prophet Isaiah, more even than the apostle Paul, interprets the Person of Christ; his is the power of seeing not with the outward eye, but with the inward vision of the spirit. In these latter chapters an alteration comes over Isaiah's picturing of the Servant of Jehovah; it is no longer a personification, but a Person; the great truth dawns on the prophet that it is God Himself in His Servant who is the Redeemer of His people.

AUGUST 22

"Despised and Rejected"

He was despised and rejected by men, a man of sorrows, and familiar with suffering. Like one from whom men hide their faces he was despised, and we esteemed him not *(Isaiah 53:3)*.

W hen Our Lord came on this earth how many discerned Him? "We needs must love the Highest when we see it"; but the highest is measured by our inner disposition, and when the Son of God, who was The Highest, appeared, men did not love Him; in fact, He was unheeded, despised, and rejected. He could easily be unheeded because He did not resent it; He could be treated like the earth under our feet. If we belong to His crowd we shall be despised. Watch how people treat you who don't love Him.

180

Preaching Christ Crucified

For I resolved to know nothing while I was with you
except Jesus Christ and him crucified *(1 Corinthians
2:2).*

"H e was despised, and we esteemed Him not." This is
God's picture of how His Servant will appear, not
sometimes, but at all times. We will preach what the apostle
Paul never preached; we will preach an exalted Christ. Paul
said, "For I determined not to know anything among you,
save Jesus Christ and Him *crucified."* Modern holiness
teachers ignore God's method and present what is called
the glory side; we have to present the side represented by
the Cross. These are all characteristics of this implicit
difference; we say, "Surely God does not mean we have to
present a despised and neglected and crucified Jesus?" He
does.

Vicarious Suffering, Realized

Surely he took up our infirmities and carried our sorrows,
yet we considered him stricken by God, smitten by him,
and afflicted *(Isaiah 53:4).*

T he coming of God is always on the line where the
devil and sin have ranged themselves—"But where
sin abounded, grace did much more abound." The
majority of people who have never been touched by
affliction see Jesus Christ's death as a thing beside the
mark; but when a man is convicted of sin, then for the first

time he begins to see something else—"At last I see, I thought He was smitted *of God;* but now I see He was wounded for *my* transgressions. he was bruised for *my* iniquities: the chastisement of *my* peace was upon Him."

AUGUST 25 _____

"Not Offended in Me"

"Blessed is the man who does not fall away on account of me" *(Matthew 11:6).*

We have the idea that prosperity, or happiness, or morality, is the end of a man's existence; according to the Bible it is something other, viz., "to glorify God and enjoy Him for ever." When a man is right with God, God puts His honour in that man's keeping. Job is one of those in whom God has staked His honour, and it was during the process of His inexplicable ways that Job makes his appeal for mercy. and yet all through there comes out his implicit confidence in God. "And blessed is he, whosoever shall not be offended in Me," said our Lord.

AUGUST 26 _____

The Trial of Your Faith

These have come so that your faith—of greater worth than gold, which perishes even though refined by fire— may be proved genuine and may result in praise, glory and honor when Jesus Christ is revealed *(1 Peter 1:7).*

The nature of faith is that it must be tested; and the trial of faith does not come in fits and starts; it goes on all the time. The one thing that keeps us right with God is the great work of His grace in our hearts. All the prophets had to take part in something they did not understand, and the Christian has to do the same. If we were to say "This is the way God is going to work," it would lead to spiritual pride, to the ban of finality about our views, to imagining that God was on our side. The question for us is, will we so yield ourselves wholly to the realization of some purpose of God? "The trial of your faith" is in order to bring God into the practical details of your life.

AUGUST 27 _____

Not a Circle But a Cross

All this is from God, who reconciled us to himself through Christ and gave us the ministry of reconciliation: that God was reconciling the world to himself in Christ, not counting men's sins against them. And he has committed to us the message of reconciliation *(2 Corinthians 5:18–19)*.

When the Bible speaks of the Death of Jesus it is not as the crucifixion of a Nazarene Carpenter, but as the point in history which reveals the nature of God—that He is not sitting on the remote circle of the world in omnipotent indifference, but that He is right at the very heart of things. The symbol for God is not a circle, but a cross, symbolic of supreme suffering and distress.

The Meaning and Cost of Forgiveness

He was oppressed and afflicted, yet he did not open his mouth; he was led like a lamb to the slaughter, and as a sheep before her shearers is silent, so he did not open his mouth. By oppression and judgment, he was taken away. And who can speak of his descendants? For he was cut off from the land of the living; for the transgression of my people he was stricken. He was assigned a grave with the wicked, and with the rich in his death, though he had done no violence, nor was any deceit in his mouth. Yet it was the LORD's will to crush him and cause him to suffer, and though the LORD makes his life a guilt offering, he will see his offspring and prolong his days, and the will of the LORD will prosper in his hand. After the suffering of his soul, he will see the light of life and be satisfied; by his knowledge my righteous servant will justify many, and he will bear their iniquities *(Isaiah 53:7–11)*.

F orgiveness of sin is the great revelation of God; all the rest is slight. We have belittled the meaning of forgiveness of *sin* by making it mean the forgiveness of offences. The only way God can forgive sin is because His Servant "poured out His soul unto death." Have I ever realized that the only way I am forgiven is by the panging depth of suffering God's Servant went through? The consciousness of what sin is comes long after the redemptive processes have been at work. The man who comes to God for the first time convicted of sins knows nothing about sin; it is the ripest saint who knows what sin is. Our salvation is the outcome of what it cost the Son of God. "He shall see of the travail of His soul, and shall be satisfied."

A Voice Brings Peace

When they had rowed three or three and a half miles, they saw Jesus approaching the boat, walking on the water; and they were terrified. But he said to them, "It is I; don't be afraid." *(John 6:19–20).*

C hildren are sometimes afraid in the dark; fear gets into their hearts and nerves and they get into a tremendous state. Then they hear the voice of mother or father and all is quietened and they go off to sleep. In our own spiritual experience it is the same; some great fear or terror comes down the road to meet us and our hearts are seized with a tremendous fear. Then we have our own name called, and the voice of Jesus saying, "It is I, be not afraid," and the peace of God which passeth all understanding takes possession of our hearts.

Forming the Mind of Christ

"By standing firm you will save yourselves" *(Luke 21:19).*

I n your patience ye shall win your souls," said Jesus to His disciples. Soul is the expression of my personal spirit in my body, the way I reason and think and act, and Jesus taught that a man must lose his soul in order to gain it; he must lose absolutely his own way of reasoning and looking at things, and begin to estimate from an entirely different standpoint. We have the Spirit of Jesus gifted to us, but we have to form the mind which was also in Christ

Jesus. No man has the mind of Christ unless he has acquired it.

AUGUST 31 _____

The Discipline of Divine Loyalty

When they had finished eating, Jesus said to Simon Peter, "Simon son of John, do you truly love me more than these?" "Yes, Lord," he said, "you know that I love you." Jesus said, "Feed my lambs." Again Jesus said, "Simon son of John, do you truly love me?" He answered, "Yes, Lord, you know that I love you." Jesus said, "Take care of of my sheep." The third time he said to him, "Simon son of John, do you love me?" Peter was hurt because Jesus asked him the third time, "Do you love me?" He said. "Lord, you know all things; you know that I love you." Jesus said, "Feed my sheep" *(John 21:15–17)*.

I s that what we have been doing, feeding Jesus Christ's sheep? Take rapid survey—have we been nourishing the lives of people in the understanding of Jesus, or has our aim been to maintain our particular deposit of doctrine? "Divine loyalty," says Jesus, "is that you feed My sheep in the knowledge of Me, not feed them with your doctrine." Peter had boasted earlier of his love for Jesus— "though all men shall be offended because of Thee, yet will I never be offended," but there is no brag left in him now— "Lord, Thou knowest all things; Thou knowest that I love Thee." "Feed My sheep." The discipline of Divine loyalty is not that I am true to a doctrine, but so true to Jesus that other people are nourished in the knowledge of Him. Get rid of the idea that you must do good things, and remember

186

what Jesus says, "If you believe on Me, out of you will flow rivers of living water." In the Christian life it is never "Do, do," but "Be, be, and I will do through you." The type of man produced by the Spirit of Jesus is the one who bears a growing family likeness to Jesus.

SEPTEMBER 1 _____

Spiritual Maturity

> Now Jesus himself was about thirty years old when he began his ministry. He was the son, so it was thought, of Joseph, the son of Heli *(Luke 3:23).*

B eing about thirty years of age . . ."—the period of maturity. Who reached maturity? The Son of God as Man, the maturity of all physical powers, all soul powers, all spiritual powers, and not until that point was reached did God thrust Him out into the three years of service. "I do always those things that are pleasing to My Father." Where did Jesus learn that power? In those thirty silent years.

Can God say of us—"That soul is learning, line upon line, precept upon precept; it is not nearly so petulant and stupid as it used to be, it no longer sulks in corners, it no longer murmurs against discipline, it is getting slowly to the place where I shall be able to do with it what I did with My own Son?"

Spiritual Freedom

> Jesus replied, "If anyone loves me, he will obey my teaching. My Father will love him, and we will come to him and make our home with him" *(John 14:23)*.

I f a man love Me, . . . he will keep My word," said Jesus; He is referring to the freedom of the disciple to keep His commandments. No natural man is free to keep the commandments of God; he is utterly unable to unless he is born again of the Holy Spirit. Freedom means ability to keep the law; every kind of freedom has to be earned. "And My Father will love him, and We will come unto him, and make Our abode with him"—an unspeakable, unstateable communion, God the Father, God the Son, and God the Holy Ghost, and the sinner saved and sanctified by grace, communing together.

His Life Laid Down, and Ours

> "The reason my Father loves me is that I lay down my life—only to take it up again. No one takes it from me, but I lay it down of my own accord. I have authority to lay it down and authority to take it up again. This command I received from my Father" *(John 10:17–18)*.

O ur Lord is referring to the power He has of Self-sacrifice. Have we that power? Thank God we have. After sanctification we have the power to deliberately take our sanctified selves and sacrifice them for God. It is an easy business to be self-sacrificing in mind—"I intend to do this and that," that is, I estimate what it is going to cost me. Paul says he not only estimated the cost, he experienced it. ". . . for Whom I suffered the loss of all things." As you go on towards maturity watch the by-path meadows—"I have been so blessed of God here; this is where I ought to stay." Read the life of Jesus; He kept His eye fixed on the one purpose His Father had for His life, which He calls "going up to Jerusalem," and we have to go with Him there.

SEPTEMBER 4 _____

"By All Means to Save Some"

> To the weak I became weak, to win the weak. I have become all things to all men so that by all possible means I might save some *(1 Corinthians 9:22)*.

A worker for God must be prepared to endure hardness; he must learn how to "sop up" all the bad and turn it into good, and nothing but the supernatural grace of God and his sense of obligation will enable him to do it. As workers we will be brought into relationship with people for whom we have no affinity; we have to stand for one thing only, "That I might by all means save some." The one mastering obligation of our life as a worker is to persuade men for Jesus Christ, and to do that we have to learn to live among facts: the fact of human stuff as it is, not as it ought to be; and the fact of Bible revelation, whether it agrees with our doctrines or not.

Are We True Prophets?

Concerning the prophets: My heart is broken within me; all my bones tremble. I am like a drunken man, like a man overcome by wine, because of the LORD and his holy words *(Jeremiah 23:9)*. *(RO*

I n chapter 23 Jeremiah speaks against the accredited leaders of the day and against the professional preachers. All that refers to the prophets of the Old Testament dispensation has a direct application to us, no matter what we think we are. The principles are for all, even the most insignificant of us. A great deal of what we proclaim can never be worked out in experience, but whenever a standard has to be proclaimed we are exonerated or condemned according to the way we carry out those dictates of the Spirit of God. We must be the living incarnation of what we teach or else we are humbugs.

The Wonder of the Child

"Why were you searching for me?" he asked. "Didn't you know I had to be in my Father's house?" *(Luke 2:49)*.

H ow is it that ye sought Me? wist ye not that I must be in My Father's house?" (v. 49). This incident is the one glimpse given to us of those twelve years so full of wonder, so full of sky-lights open towards God. Think of the pure wonder of the Child Jesus in the temple when He realized with spiritual intuition that He was in His Father's

House; don't picture a precocious intellectual prig, Jesus was amazed that His Mother did not know what He knew, or understand what He understood. A child's mind exhibits the innocence of intelligence, and in the life of Jesus this innocence never became conceited.

The Value of the Waiting Time

Then he went down to Nazareth with them and was obedient to them. But his mother treasured all these things in her heart *(Luke 2:51)*.

A nd He was subject unto them" (v. 51). Have we ever caught the full force of the thirty silent years, of those three years wandering in Palestine? Have we ever caught the full force of those ten days of waiting in the upper room? If we measure those periods by our modern way of estimating we will put it down as waste of time; but into the life of Our Lord, into the lives of the early disciples, were going to come elements that would root and ground them on a solid foundation that nothing could shake. The waiting time is always the testing time.

The Saints' Reaction to Suffering

Therefore we do not lose heart. Though outwardly we are wasting away, yet inwardly we are being renewed day by day. For our light and momentary troubles are achieving for us an eternal glory that far outweighs them all *(2 Corinthians 4:16–17)*.

The evident indifference on the part of the saints in the New Testament, and since, to the experience of suffering is accounted for, not on the ground of insensitiveness or by tramping on the finer feelings, but by the "expulsive power of a new affection." When we are saved and sanctified through the Atonement we are led out into the fulfillment of the ideas of God under the Lordship of Jesus Christ. Every other aim falls into insignificance; and through earth's heartbreaks, sorrows, and griefs, the sanctified soul treads calm and unwavering, unafraid even of death itself, summing up all as "our light affliction, which is for the moment . . ."

SEPTEMBER 9 _____

The Peril of Reformation

"When an evil spirit comes out of a man, it goes through arid places seeking rest and does not find it. Then it says, 'I will return to the house I left' " *(Luke 11:24)*.

Luke 11:24 is a picture of clear sweeping reformation, the house "swept and garnished"; but our Lord is pointing out in the parable the peril of a moral victory unused because the heart is left empty. The man who reforms without any knowledge of the grace of God is the subtlest infidel with regard to the need of regeneration. It is a good thing to have the heart swept, but it becomes the worst thing if the heart is left vacant for spirits more evil than itself to enter; Jesus says that "the last state of that man becometh worse than the first." Reformation is a good thing, but like every other good thing it is the enemy of the best. Regeneration means filling the heart with something positive, viz., the Holy Spirit (Luke 11:13).

SEPTEMBER 10

Remorse Not Repentance

> Then the LORD said to Cain, "Where is your brother Abel?" "I don't know," he replied. "Am I my brother's keeper?" The LORD said, "What have you done? Listen! Your brother's blood cries out to me from the ground. Now you are under a curse and driven from the ground, which opened its mouth to receive your brother's blood from your hand. When you work the ground, it will no longer yield its crops for you. You will be a restless wanderer on the earth." Cain said to the LORD , "My punishment is more that I can bear. Today you are driving me from the land, and I will be hidden from your presence; I will be a restless wanderer on the earth, and whoever finds me will kill me" *(Genesis 4:9–14).*

> So Judas threw the money into the temple and left. Then he went away and hanged himself *(Matthew 27:5).*

N ever mistake remorse for repentance; remorse simply puts a man in hell while he is on earth; it carries no remedial quality with it at all, nothing that betters a man. An unawakened sinner has no remorse, but immediately a man recognizes his sin he experiences the pain of being gnawed by a sense of guilt, for which punishment would be a heaven of relief, but no punishment can touch it. In the case of Cain (see Genesis 4:9–14) remorse is seen at its height: "Mine iniquity is greater than can be forgiven" (v 13, R.V. marg.). Cain was in the condition of being found out by his own sin; his conscience recognized what he had done, and he knew that God recognized it too.

Expansion Demands Expression

Therefore, my dear friends, as you have always obeyed—not only in my presence, but now much more in my absence—continue to work out your salvation with fear and trembling, for it is God who works in you to will and to act according to his good purpose *(Philippians 2:12–13).*

When God gives a vision of what sanctification means, or what the life of faith means, we have instantly to pay for the vision, and we pay for it by the inevitable law that "expansion must be followed by concentration." That means we must concentrate on the vision until it becomes real. Over and over again the vision is mistaken for the reality. God's great Divine anticipation can only be made manifest by our human participation; these two must not be put asunder. Every expansion of brain and heart that God gives in meetings or in private reading of the Bible must be paid for inevitably and inexorably by concentration on our part, not by consecration. God will continually bring us into circumstances to make us prove whether we will work out with determined concentration what He has worked in.

Faith Claims the Whole Man

And without faith it is impossible to please God, because anyone who comes to him must believe that he exists and that he rewards those who earnestly seek him (Hebrews 11:6).

F aith is not a faculty; faith is the whole man rightly related to God by the power of the Spirit of Jesus. We are apt to apply faith to certain domains of our lives only; e.g., we have faith in God when we ask Him to save us, or ask Him for the Holy Spirit, but we trust something other than God in the actual details of our lives. "Faith claims the whole man and all that God's grace can make him," just as it claimed the whole of our Lord's life. Our Lord represents the normal man, not the average man, but the man according to God's norm; His life was not cut up into compartments, one part sacred and another secular; it was not in any way a mutilated life. Jesus Christ was concentrated on one line, viz., the will of His Father, in every detail of His life.

Under Divine Orders

And you are of Christ, and Christ is of God (1 Corinthians 3:23).

"You call me 'Teacher' and 'Lord,' and rightly so, for that is what I am" (John 13:13).

I f for one whole day, quietly and determinedly, we were to give ourselves up to the ownership of Jesus and to obeying His orders, we should be amazed at its close to realize all He had packed into that one day. We say— "Oh, but I have a special work to do." No Christian has a special work to do. A Christian is called to be Jesus Christ's own, one chosen by Him; one who is not above his Master, and who does not dictate to Jesus as to what he intends to do. Our Lord calls to no special work; He calls to Himself. Pray to the Lord of the harvest, and He will engineer your circumstances and thrust you out.

SEPTEMBER 14 _____

The Missionary's Secret

" 'Now get up and stand on your feet. I have appeared to you to appoint you as a servant and as a witness of what you have seen of me and what I will show you. I will rescue you from your own people and from the Gentiles. I am sending you to open their eyes and turn them from darkness to light, and from the power of Satan to God, so that they may receive forgiveness of sins and a place among those who are sanctified by faith in me' " *(Acts 26:16–18)*.

The great Author and Originator of all missionary enterprise is God, and we must keep in touch with His line. The call to the missionary does not arise out of the discernment of his own mind, or from the sympathy of his own heart, but because behind the face of every downtrodden heathen, he sees the face of Jesus Christ, and hears His command—"Go ye therefore, and make disciples of all the nations." The need of the heathen world can only be met by our Risen Lord who has all power in heaven and in

196

earth, and by our receiving from Him the enduement of power from on high.

_____

Going Up to Jerusalem

As the time approached for him to be taken up to heaven, Jesus resolutely set out for Jerusalem *(Luke 9:51)*.

T he New Testament centers round one Person, the Lord Jesus Christ. We are regenerated into His Kingdom by means of His Cross, and then we go up to our Jerusalem, having His Life as our example. We must be born from above before we can go up to our Jerusalem, and the things He met with on His way will throw a flood of light on the things we shall meet with. Our Jerusalem means the place where we reach the climax of Our Lord's will for us, which is that we may be made one with Him as He is one with the Father.

_____

The Passion of the Sanctified

May God himself, the God of peace, sanctify you through and through. May your whole spirit, soul and body be kept blameless at the coming of our Lord Jesus Christ *(1 Thessalonians 5:23)*.

A child in the natural world is not fit for life unless it is perfectly healthy; sanctification is spiritual health, "perfect soundness." May the God of peace sanctify us wholly so that we are no longer sickly souls retarding His purposes, but "perfected through suffering." Oh, that from every heart may rise the yearning longing as from the apostle Paul:

Then as I weary me and long and languish,
Nowise availing from that pain to part,—
Desperate tides of the whole great world's anguish
Forced thro' the channels of a single heart.

Oh to save these! to perish for their saving,
Die for their life, be offered for them all!

SEPTEMBER 17 _____

The Upward Look

I lift up my eyes to the hills—where does my help come from? *(Psalm 121:1).*

Psalm 121:1 portrays well the upward look—"Shall I lift up mine eyes to the hills? from whence should my help come? My help cometh from the Lord, which made heaven and earth." The upward look of a mature man of God is not to the mountains which God has made, but to the God who made the mountains. It is the maintained set of the highest powers of a man—not stargazing till you stumble, but the upward gaze deliberately set towards God. He has got through the "choppy waters" of his elementary spiritual experience and now he is set on God; but you have to fight for it. "I have set the Lord always before me," said the Psalmist. Our Lord presents the upward look to the last degree of perfection.

The Forward Look

Your eyes will see the king in his beauty and view a land that stretches afar *(Isaiah 33:17)*.

T hine eyes shall see the king in His beauty: they shall behold a far stretching land"—("a land of far distances," marg.) The forward look is the look that sees everything in God's perspective whereby His wonderful distance is put on the things that are nearest. Caleb had the perspective of God; the men who went up with him saw only the inhabitants as giants and themselves as grass-hoppers. Learn to take the long view and you will breathe the benediction of God among the squalid things that surround you. Some people never get ordinary or com-monplace; they transfigure everything they touch because they have got the forward look which brings confidence in God into their actual life.

Human Nature and Holiness

Therefore do not let sin reign in your mortal body so that you obey its evil desires. Do not offer the parts of your body to sin, as instruments of wickedness, but rather offer yourselves to God, as those who have been brought from death to life; and offer the parts of your body to him as instruments of righteousness. For sin shall not be your master, because you are not under law, but under grace. What then? Shall we sin because we are not under law but under grace? By no means! Don't you know that when you offer yourselves to someone to obey him as slaves, you are slaves to the one whom you obey—whether you are slaves to sin, which leads to death, or to obedience, which leads to righteousness? But thanks be to God that, though you used to be slaves to sin, you wholeheartedly obeyed the form of teaching to which you were entrusted. You have been set free from sin and have become slaves to righteousness. I put this in human terms because you are weak in your natural selves. Just as you used to offer the parts of your body in slavery to impurity and to ever-increasing wickedness, so now offer them in slavery to righteousness leading to holiness *(Romans 6:12–19)*.

When I am born again my human nature is not different, it is the same as before; I am related to life in the same way, I have the same bodily organs, but the mainspring is different, and I have to see now that I am dominated by the new disposition (see Romans 6:13, 19). You cannot live the life God wants you to live as a saint unless you remain the man or woman God meant you to be. There is only one kind of human nature, and that is the human nature we have all got; there is only one kind of holiness, and that is the holiness of Jesus Christ. Give Him "elbow room," and He will manifest Himself in you, and other people will recognize Him.

SEPTEMBER 20 _____

Offended With Jesus?

From this time many of his disciples turned back and no longer followed him *(John 6:66)*.

The crowds have passed now, you are alone with your Lord, and He bends through the gloom of your weakness and blindness and says "You are not going away too, are you?"

Men are still offended at Jesus; they hear gladly His "Follow Me" and enthusiastically leave all to follow, but when the way becomes narrow, and to follow costs shedding of blood, they begin to waver. As long as it means peace and joy we will follow Jesus, but when it costs us dear we are tempted to go back and walk no more with Him.

SEPTEMBER 21 _____

The Power of the Blood

> Jesus said to them, "I tell you the truth, unless you eat the flesh of the Son of Man and drink his blood, you have no life in you. Whoever eats my flesh and drinks my blood has eternal life, and I will raise him up at the last day. For my flesh is real food and my blood is real drink. Whoever eats my flesh and drinks my blood remains in me, and I in him" *(John 6:53–56).*

B lood" is an offence not only at the beginning of the Christian career, but in the midst of it. "Except ye eat the flesh of the Son of Man, and drink His blood, ye have no life in you." . . . "Doth this offend you?" said Jesus— "Except you are crucified with Christ until all that is left is the life of Christ in your flesh and blood, *you have no life in you.*" "Except your self-love is flooded away by the inrush of the love of Jesus so that you feel your blood move through you in tender charity as it moved through Him, *you have no life in you.*" "Except your flesh becomes the temple of His holiness and you abide in Christ and He in you, *you have no life in you.*"

201

The Sentence of Death

Indeed, in our hearts we felt the sentence of death. But this happened that we might not rely on ourselves but on God, who raises the dead *(2 Corinthians 1:9).*

I f I am in fellowship with Jesus Christ and am indwelt by Him, I have the answer of death in myself, and nothing the world, the flesh, or the devil can do can touch me. This divine light came to Paul out of his desperate experience in Ephesus; he realized then that nothing could any more affright him. The discipline of fellowship brought about in Paul's experience the assimilation of what he believed. We say many things which we believe, but they have never been tested. Discipline has to come through all the things we believe in order to turn them into real spiritual possessions. It is the trial of our faith that is precious. "Hang in" to Jesus Christ against all odds until He turns your spiritual beliefs into real possessions. It is heroism to believe in God.

Jesus Understands the Power of Our Enemy

"Simon, Simon, Satan has asked to sift you as wheat. But I have prayed for you, Simon, that your faith may not fail. And when you have turned back, strengthen your brothers" *(Luke 22:31–32).*

P eter loved Jesus Christ and declared that he was ready to lay down his life for Him, and yet he denied Him thrice with oaths and curses. But Jesus never lost heart over him; He told him beforehand—". . . but I made supplication for thee, that thy faith fail not; and do thou, when once thou has turned again, stablish thy brethren." Sin never once frightened Jesus; the devil never once frightened Him. Face the devil with all the power of Jesus Christ: "He was manifested, that He might *destroy the works of the devil."* Are you being tripped up by the subtle power of the devil? Remember, Jesus Christ has power not only to release you, but to make you more than conqueror over all the devil's onslaughts.

SEPTEMBER 24

More Than a Sympathizer, a Saviour

The scroll of the prophet Isaiah was handed to him. Unrolling it, he found the place where it is written: "The Spirit of the Lord is on me, because he has anointed me to preach good news to the poor. He has sent me to proclaim freedom for the prisoners and recovery of sight for the blind, to release the oppressed, to proclaim the year of the Lord's favor" *(Luke 4:17–19).*

To picture Jesus Christ, never so beautifully, as One who sits down beside the brokenhearted and by expression of fellow-feeling and overflowing tenderness, enables him to be resigned and submissive to his lot, is not only thoroughly to misunderstand our Lord, but to prevent Him doing what He came to do. He does come to the brokenhearted, to the captives bound by a cursed heredi- tary tendency, to the blind who grope for light, to the man bruised and crushed by his surroundings, but He does not come as a sympathizer—He "binds up the brokenhearted, gives release to the captives, recovering of sight to the blind;

203

He sets at liberty them that are bruised." Jesus Christ is not a mere sympathizer; He is a Saviour, and the only One.

The Altar of Fellowship

So I will very gladly spend for you everything I have and expend myself as well. If I love you more, will you love me less? *(2 Corinthians 12:15)*.

H uman fellowship can go to great lengths, but not all the way. Fellowship with God can go all lengths. The apostle Paul literally fulfilled what we mean by this phrase, the altar of fellowship; he offered himself liberally and freely to God, and then offered himself at the hands of God, freely and fully, for the service of God among men, whether or not men understood him. "And I will very gladly spend and be spent for you; though the more abundantly I love you, the less I be loved." Do we know anything about this altar of fellowship whereby we offer back to God the best He has given us, and then let Him re-offer it as broken bread and poured-out wine to His other children?

Prayer on the Right Basis

After they prayed, the place where they were meeting was shaken. And they were all filled with the Holy Spirit and spoke the word of God boldly *(Acts 4:31)*.

H ow strongly spiritual efficacy in prayer is marked all through the Acts of the apostles! It is the sign Jesus

Christ gives that we believe in Him (see John 14:12–13). Prayer that is not saturated in the New Testament is apt to be based on human earnestness. God never hears prayer because a man is in earnest; He hears and answers prayer that is on the right platform—we have "boldness to enter into the holy place *by the blood of Jesus,*" and by no other way. It is not our agony and our distress, but our childlike confidence in God.

SEPTEMBER 27

The Liberated Preacher

"Go, stand in the temple courts," he said, "and tell the people the full message of this new life" *(Acts 5:20).*

U nless a preacher has had a saving experience, i.e., been set free from some "prison," he has not got God's "go" in him. If this test were put to every preacher and Sunday school teacher—Has Jesus Christ done anything for you you could not do for yourself? Has He set you free from the "prison" of a wrong disposition, set you free from the tyranny of nerves? from pride? from a wrong mental outlook?—the result straightaway would be to thin the number of those who are at work for God, and those that were left would be the men of God's method. The man of God's method says—"I know I have been delivered by God; I don't know *how* He did it, but I know He did it."

Christ's Knowledge of the Human Heart

"For out of the heart come evil thoughts, murder, adultery, sexual immorality, theft, false testimony, slander" *(Matthew 15:19).*

J esus Christ treated men from the standpoint of His certain knowledge of them; He is the supreme Master of the human heart. Recall what He said—"for from within, out of the heart of man, proceed . . . "; consequently He was never surprised, never in a panic. When He met the rich young ruler, an upright-living splendid young man, we read that "Jesus looking upon him loved him." Jesus Christ loved morality, but He never said it was enough. "If thou wilt be perfect . . ." then come the conditions; Jesus knew that at the back of the natural virtues was a disposition that could willfully sin against God. Again when He met Nicodemus, a godly man, a ruler of the synagogue, He told him he must be made all over again before he could enter the kingdom of God.

"Having Done All, to Stand"

Therefore put on the full armor of God, so that when the day of evil comes, you may be able to stand your ground, and after you have done everything to stand *(Ephesians 6:13).*

I t takes a tremendously strong man to stand—"and, having done all, to stand." Not fight, but stand. The men of God's method are never hustled, never enticed;

they won't allow themselves to be deflected, they know what they are there for. "None of these things move me," said Paul, "you may execrate me, or praise me, it makes no difference; I am here for only one thing—to fulfill the ministry which I received from the Lord Jesus."

SEPTEMBER 30

What Do You Know?

Jesus knew that the Father had put all things under his power, and that he had come from God and was returning to God; so he got up from the meal, took off his outer clothing, and wrapped a towel around his waist *(John 13:3–4).*

J esus knowing . . . that He was come from God . . ." Do you know that you have received the Holy Spirit, know that you are a child of God—are you going to be greater that Jesus Christ? Are you going to be disdainful—" What a humiliating thing to do!" Jesus, knowing who He was, took a towel and washed the disciples' feet; and He says, "I have given you an example, that ye should do as I have done to you." To shout "Hallelujah" is humbug unless it is genuine. Jesus never tells you to shout "Hallelujah": He says—*"Do as I have done to you."* How much long-suffering mercy has God shown you?

OCTOBER 1 _____

The Witness of Sorrow

> Then the man in linen with the writing kit at his side
> brought back word, saying, "I have done as you
> commanded" *(Ezekiel 9:11)*.

I n this ancient book of Ezekiel the man clothed in
linen, with a writer's inkhorn by his side, was to set a
mark upon the foreheads of the men who sorrowed for the
city's sin. Let us take time to wonder if such a visitant on
such an errand would mark us as among the people
privileged to sorrow thus. Jeremiah has been called "the
weeping prophet," and in his Lamentations we find that the
secret of his sorrow is Jerusalem, the city of his love. "How
doth the city sit solitary, that was full of people!" (1:1).
Instantly our minds pass on to what is recorded in Luke
19:41, "And when He drew nigh, He saw the city and wept
over it," and we remember with adoring wonder that Our
Lord is known throughout all generations as "a Man of
sorrows."

OCTOBER 2 _____

Worldly Sorrow

> Godly sorrow brings repentance that leads to salvation
> and leaves no regret, but worldly sorrow brings death"
> *(2 Corinthians 7:10)*.

I t is a terrible thing to say, and yet true, that there is a
sorrow so selfish, so sentimental and sarcastic that it
adds to the sin of the city. All sorrow that arises from being
baffled in some selfish aim of our own is of the world and

works death. Those who sorrow over their own weaknesses and sins and stop short at that, have a sorrow that only makes them worse; it is not a godly sorrow that works repentance. Oh that all men knew that every sentiment has its appropriate reaction, and if the nature does not embrace that reaction it degenerates into a sullen sentimentalism that kills all good action.

OCTOBER 3

Fruitful Sorrow

"Is it nothing to you, all you who pass by? Look around and see. Is any suffering like my suffering that was inflicted on me, that the LORD brought on me in the day of his fierce anger?" *(Lamentations 1:12)*.

T he sign for the world without God is a circle, complete in and for itself; the sign for the Christian is the Cross. The Christian knows by bitter yet blessed conviction of sin that no man is sufficient for himself, and he thereby enters into identification with the Cross of Calvary, and he longs and prays and works to see the sinful, self-centered world broken up and made the occasion for the mighty Cross to have its way whereby men may come to God and God come down to men.

OCTOBER 4

Failure in Sorrow

Then he returned to his disciples and found them sleeping. "Could you men not keep watch with me for one hour?" he asked Peter *(Matthew 26:40)*.

That is why many among you are weak and sick, and a number of you have fallen asleep *(1 Corinthians 11:30).*

There are many to-day who are suffering from spiritual sleeping sickness, and the sorrow of the world which works death is witnessed in all directions. If personal sorrow does not work itself out along the appropriate line, it will lull us to a pessimistic sleep. For instance, when we see our brother "sinning a sin not unto death," do we get to prayer for him, probed by the searching sorrow of his sin? (see 1 John 5:16).

OCTOBER 5 _____

No Second Causes

Jesus answered, "You would have no power over me if it were not given to you from above. Therefore the one who handed me over to you is guilty of a greater sin" *(John 19:11).*

We are too shallow to be afraid of God. All the Hebrew prophets reveal this truth, that there is only one Cause and no "second causes." It requires a miracle of grace before we believe this; consequently we are foolishly fearless, but when the grace of God lifts us into the life of God we fear nothing and no one saving God alone. The "no second causes" truth was ever apparent to Our Lord; e.g., "Thou couldest have no power at all against Me, except it were given thee from above."

God's Inexorable Demands

Make every effort to live in peace with all men and to be holy; without holiness no one will see the Lord *(Hebrews 12:14)*.

I f my first step has not been one of penitential repentance I will at one time meet the "artillery" of God and down I go, no matter how earnestly I pray and mouth my testimony, for this reason—God will have nothing in His Presence but holiness and uprightness and integrity. "Those things will never happen to me, there are circumstances in my case which exonerate"; there are not. God's demands are inexorable; only one thing will satisfy Him, and that is speckless, spotless holiness, and He will never let us go until He has brought us there—unless we wrest ourselves out of His hand.

The Only Way

Jesus answered, "I am the way and the truth and the life. No one comes to the Father except through me" *(John 14:6)*.

I am the Way"—God has no other Way. Jesus Christ is the only Way in every profound problem; the reason we can do without Him is that we have not come up against profound things. We may have a vivid religious experience and yet not think along Christian lines. All things are not black or white, right or wrong; there is no problem about right and wrong, these things are clearly marked. But there are things that are perplexing: Is Jesus Christ "the Way" in those? We are apt to get impatient with the things that are obscure and difficult to decipher.

_____

All Things . . . to the Lord

Whatever you do, work at it with all your heart, as working for the Lord, not for men (Colossians 3:23).

I f there is anything in my life in which I have to justify myself, I am not walking in the light.

Beware of being negligent in some lesser thing while being good in a greater thing; e.g., I may be good in a prayer meeting but not good in the matter of cleaning my boots. It is a real peril, and springs from selecting some one thing our Lord taught as our standard instead of God Himself.

_____

The Lion Lamb

And when he had taken it, the four living creatures and the twenty-four elders fell down before the Lamb. Each one had a harp and they were holding golden bowls full of incense, which are the prayers of the saints (Revelation 5:8).

I n the days of His flesh Jesus Christ exhibited this Divine paradox of the Lion and the Lamb—He was the Lion in majesty, rebuking winds and demons: He was the Lamb in meekness, "who when He was reviled, reviled not again." He was the Lion in power, raising Lazarus and others from the dead: He was the Lamb in patience, who was "brought as a lamb to the slaughter, and as a sheep before her shearers is dumb, so He openeth not his mouth." He was the Lion in authority—"Ye have heard that it was said, . . . but *I* say unto you: . . ." He was the Lamb in gentleness, taking little children up in His arms and saying "Suffer little children, and forbid them not, to come unto Me."

OCTOBER 10 _____

The Vine—for Fruit or Fire

"I am the vine; you are the branches. If a man remains in me and I in him, he will bear much fruit; apart from me you can do nothing. If anyone does not remain in me, he is like a branch that is thrown away and withers; such branches are picked up, thrown into the fire and burned" *(John 15:5–6)*. (

T he vine is of no value if it is not fruitful; trees which are not fruit-bearing are excellent for other purposes, but not so the vine which is fit only for fruit or for fire. What God burns is not weakness, not imperfection, but perverted goodness. Fruit is the manifestation of the essential nature of the tree, and our human lives are meant to bring forth the fruit of the Spirit, which is, literally, the life of God in me, invading me, producing fruit for His glory. "Herein is My Father glorified, that ye bear much fruit."

⎯⎯⎯⎯⎯⎯⎯⎯⎯⎯⎯⎯⎯

The Divine Withdrawal

I opened for my lover, but my lover had left; he was gone. My heart had gone out to him when he spoke. I looked for him but did not find him. I called him but he did not answer *(Song of Songs 5:6)*.

I nterior desolation serves a vital purpose in the life of a Christian. At the beginning of the spiritual life the consciousness of God is so wonderful that we are apt to imagine our communion with God depends upon our being conscious of His presence. Then when God begins to withdraw us into Himself and things become mysterious, we lose our faith and get into the dark, and say—"I must have backslidden," and yet we know we have not; all we know is that we have lost our consciousness of God's presence.

OCTOBER 12 ⎯⎯⎯⎯⎯⎯⎯⎯⎯⎯⎯⎯⎯

Making the Natural Spiritual

Do you not know that your body is a temple of the Holy Spirit, who is in you, whom you have received from God? You are not your own *(1 Corinthians 6:19)*.

E very part of our human nature which is not brought into subjection to the Holy Spirit after experiencing deliverance from sin will prove a corrupting influence. We are not delivered from human nature; human nature was created by God, not by the devil; it is impaired, and enfeebled, but it is not sinful. The first creation retains the remnants of God's handiwork; re-creation is the building of

214

a spiritual habitation, "an habitation of God," and all our effort is to be spent in disciplining the natural life in obedience to the new creation wrought in us through the Spirit. If I refuse to make my natural life spiritual by the slow process of obedience, my religious profession becomes a disgusting hypocrisy.

OCTOBER 13

Climate and Character

He got up, rebuked the wind and said to the waves, "Quiet! Be still!" Then the wind died down and it was completely calm *(Mark 4:39)*.

T he life of Our Lord exhibits the influence of character on climate. It is easy to make this absurd, but looked at from the attitude of the Spirit of God you find there is an amazing connection between the storm and distresses and wild confusion of the earth just now and the waywardness and wrong of man; when the waywardness of man ceases and the sons of God are manifested then "the creature itself also shall be delivered from the bondage of corruption into the glorious liberty of the children of God."

OCTOBER 14

Communion at Daybreak

One of those days Jesus went out into the hills to pray, and spent the night praying to God. When morning came, he called his disciples to him and chose twelve of them, whom he also designated apostles *(Luke 6:12– 13)*.

I t is not a haphazard thing, but in the constitution of God, that there are certain times of the day when it not only seems easier, but it *is* easier, to meet God. If you have ever prayed in the dawn you will ask yourself why you were so foolish as not to do it always. It is difficult to get into communion with God in the midst of the hurly-burly of the day. It is not sentiment but an implicit reality that the conditions of dawn and communion with God go together. When the day of God appears there will be no night, always dawn and day. There is nothing of the nature of strain in God's Day; it is all free and beautiful and fine.

_____

The Source and the Outflow

"Whoever believes in me, as the Scripture has said, streams of living water will flow from within him" *(John 7:38).*

J esus did not say, "He that believeth on Me, shall experience the fulness of the blessing of God"; but, "he that believeth on Me, out of him shall escape everything he receives." It is a picture of the unfathomable, incalculable benediction which will flow from the one great sovereign Source, belief in Jesus. We have nothing to do with the outflow; we have to see to it that we are destitute enough of spiritual independence to be filled with the Holy Ghost and then pay attention to the Source Our Lord Himself. You can never measure what God will do through you if you are rightly related to Jesus. The parenthesis in v. 39 does not apply to us: the Holy Ghost *has been* given; Jesus *is* glorified; the rivers of living water are there, and, unspeakable wonder! the sacrament may flow through our lives too. All that the one out of whom the river of living water are flowing is conscious of is belief in Jesus and maintaining a right relationship to Him; then day by day God is pouring the rivers of living water through you, and it is of His mercy He does not let you know it.

OCTOBER 16 _____

Wrath or Love?

But because of your stubbornness and your unrepentant heart, you are storing up wrath against yourself for the day of God's wrath, when his righteous judgment will be revealed *(Romans 2:5).*

And we know that in all things God works for the good of those who love him, who have been called according to his purpose *(Romans 8:28).*

When our supreme temptation comes, the setting we are in, whether it is a city or the actual desert, brings us into contact with the foundation of things as God made them. According to Genesis, the basis of physical material life is chaos, and the basis of personal moral life, wrath. If I live in harmony with God, chaos becomes cosmos to me, and the wrath of God becomes the love of God. If I get out of touch with God I get into hell, physically and morally; when I live in relationship to God by the inner witness of the Spirit, "Heaven above is brighter blue, earth around a sweeter green . . ."

217

The Desperation of a Disciple

"Simon, Simon, Satan has asked to sift you as wheat. But I have prayed for you, Simon, that your faith may not fail. And when you have turned back, strengthen your brothers" *(Luke 22:31–32)*.

T he devil tried to get Peter where he got Judas, but he did not succeed; Satan did not "enter into" Peter; Peter got the length of denying Jesus, but in his wilderness of temptation he "struck" the Divine; consequently Peter experienced a desperation producing tears, and those tears were the most amazing bitterness in his life. Peter with his impulsive heart would feel he could never forgive himself; he would have spent the rest of his days mourning, but Jesus had told him beforehand, "And do thou, when once thou hast turned again, establish thy brethren."

God's Love in Our Hearts

"I have made you known to them, and will continue to make you known in order that the love you have for me may be in them and that I myself may be in them" *(John 17:26)*.

R ecall to your mind the touchings of the love of God in your life, and you will never find it difficult to do anything He says. It is not your power of loving God that enables you to do it; it is the presence of the very nature of God in your heart that makes it so easy to obey Him that you don't know you are obeying Him. Never quench that spirit.

OCTOBER 19 _____

A Deserved Rebuke

He said to his disciples, "Why are you so afraid? Do you still have no faith?" *(Mark 4:40)*.

Our Lord rebuked the disciples for fearing when apparently they had good reason for being alarmed. The problem is—if Jesus Christ is only the Carpenter of Nazareth, then the disciples were foolish to put Him at the tiller; but if He is the Son of God, what are they alarmed about? If Jesus Christ is God, where is my trust in Him? If He is not God, why am I so foolish as to pretend to worship Him? "And they feared exceedingly, and said one to another, What manner of man is this, that even the wind and the sea obey Him?"

OCTOBER 20 _____

Faith Tested in the Storm

Therefore we will not fear, though the earth give way and the mountains fall into the heart of the sea, though its waters roar and foam and the mountains quake with their surging *(Psalm 46:2–3)*.

God engineers us out of the sequestered places and brings us into elemental conditions and we get a taste of what the world is like because of the disobedience of man. We realize then that our hold on God has been a civilized hold; we have not really believed in Him at all. When we get out on to the deep and the darkness we realize what a wonderful thing the Psalmist says—"Therefore will we not fear, though the earth be removed . . ." But it takes some confidence in God to say that when everything you trust in has gone.

OCTOBER 21 _____

Confidence Amid World Trouble

"When you hear of wars and rumors of wars, do not be alarmed. Such things must happen, but the end is still to come" *(Mark 13:7).*

J esus Christ teaches us to build our confidence in the abiding reality of Himself in the midst of everything. If a man puts his confidence in the things which must go, imagine his incomprehensible perplexity when they do go. No wonder Jesus said "men's hearts fail in them for fear." These words describe the time we are in now. But to His disciples Jesus said, "When *you* hear of wars and rumors of wars, see that ye be not troubled." Our true life is not in the things which are passing, and if we build ourselves on God and His Word, when they go, the marvel is that we are not scared. The thing to examine spiritually is, am I connected with Jesus Christ personally?

OCTOBER 22 _____

The Evangel More Than Ethics

"Be perfect, therefore, as your heavenly Father is perfect" *(Matthew 5:48).*

Wherever Christianity has ceased to be vigorous it is because it has become Christian *ethics* instead of the Christian *evangel*. People will listen more readily to an exposition of the Sermon on the Mount than they will to the meaning of the Cross; but they forget that to preach the Sermon on the Mount apart from the Cross is to preach an impossibility. What is the good of telling me to love my enemies—and "Blessed are the pure in heart"? You may talk like that to further orders, but it does not amount to anything. Jesus Christ did not come to teach men to do any of these things—He did not come primarily to teach; He came to make a man the possessor of His own disposition, the disposition which is portrayed in the Sermon on the Mount.

OCTOBER 23 _____

The Blessing of the Unnoticed

Whatever you do, work at it with all your heart, as working for the Lord, not for men *(Colossians 3:23)*.

If you are rightly devoted to Jesus Christ, you have reached the sublime height where no one thinks of noticing you; all that is noticed is that the power of God comes through all the time. It is along some such line as this that we are to understand the omniscience of God and human life. "I have had a wonderful call from God!" It takes Almighty God Incarnate in you to peel potatoes properly, and to wash heathen children for the glory of God. *Anyone* cannot do these things; anybody can do the shining in the sun and the sporting in the footlights, but it

221

takes God's Incarnated Spirit to make you so absolutely humanly His that you are utterly unnoticeable.

God's Forgiveness and Ours

"For if you forgive men when they sin against you, your heavenly Father will also forgive you" *(Matthew 6:14).*

A self indwelt by Jesus becomes like Him. "Walk in love, even as Christ also loved you." Jesus has loved me to the end of all my meanness and selfishness and sin; now, He says, show that same love to others. "For if ye forgive men their trespasses, your heavenly Father will also forgive you,"—that is, I am to ask to be forgiven, not on the ground of the Atonement, but because I forgive. "But if ye forgive not men their trespasses, neither will your Father forgive your trespasses." That is hard hitting. Am I prepared to show the man who does evil to me the love God has shown to me? I have to learn to identify myself with God's interests in other people, and God's interests are never my selfish interests.

Helping Others Through the Straight Gate

"Make every effort to enter through the narrow door, because many, I tell you, will try to enter and will not be able to" *(Luke 13:24).*

S truggle to gain the mastery over selfishness, and you will be a tremendous assistance; but if you don't overcome the tendency to spiritual sluggishness and self-indulgence, you are a hindrance to all around you. These things are intangible, but they are there, and Jesus says to us, "Strive to enter in at the strait gate." You never get through alone. If you struggle to get through, others are the stronger and better for knowing you. The men and women who lift and inspire us are those who struggle for self, not for self-assertiveness, that is a sign of weakness, but for the development of personality. There are some people in whose company you cannot have a mean thought without being instantly rebuked.

OCTOBER 26

God's In-working and Our Out-working

Therefore, my dear friends, as you have always obeyed—not only in my presence, but now much more in my absence—continue to work out your salvation with fear and trembling, for it is God who works in you to will and to act according to his good purpose *(Philippians 2:12–13)*.

"O wretched man that I am! who shall deliver me from this chronic incapacity? I consent that a thing is right and yet I do the wrong." When the Holy Spirit comes in He energizes a man's will; He works in him to will to want to do the will of God. The deliverance is a very profound and practical one; God alters my "want to," i.e., the ruling disposition, by introducing His own will into me. Now, says the apostle, work out your own salvation—if you are saved, exhibit it in your practical life, manifest the heavenly disposition in your home, in your business.

223

Defeat in the Desert

Then the devil left him, and angels came and attended him *(Matthew 4:11)*.

J esus Christ met the devil in the wilderness and defeated Him. When you go through a time of trial, a wilderness of temptation in heart or mind or spirit, you feel inclined to get away out into somewhere like the desert. The reason for that is not haphazard, but because in the primal constitution of God man is connected with the dust of the earth. He is related to the elemental condition of things all through. When the sons of God are manifested the desolate place will alter at once. "The desert shall rejoice, and blossom as the rose."

Personality Split Through Sin

As it is, it is no longer I myself who do it, but it is sin living in me. I know that nothing good lives in me, that is, in my sinful nature. For I have the desire to do what is good, but I cannot carry it out. For what I do is not the good I want to do; no, the evil I do not want to do—this I keep on doing. Now if I do what I do not want to do, it is no longer I who do it, but it is sin living in me that does it. So I find this law at work: When I want to do good, evil is right there with me. For in my inner being I delight in God's law; but I see another law at work in the members of my body, waging war against the law of my mind and making me a prisoner of the law of sin at work within my members. What a wretched man I am! Who will rescue me from this body of death? Thanks be to God—through Jesus Christ our Lord! So then, I myself in my mind am a slave to God's law, but in the sinful nature a slave to the law of sin *(Romans 7:17–25)*.

R omans 7 is the classic for all time of the tragedy of a man whose mind is awakened by the incoming of the disturbing nature of God (see vv. 7–11). The incoming of the Holy Spirit into a man results sooner or later in the splitting up of personal unity into conscious conflict. There is no real spiritual stability, no spiritual triumph. Sin has so thwarted a man's personality that he has no power over it—"sold under sin"—there are things that make me do what I don't want to. The only One who can deliver him is Jesus Christ. That is the apostle's contention all through— "I thank God through Jesus Christ our Lord . . . For the law of the Spirit of life in Christ Jesus *hath made me free* from the law of sin and of death."

OCTOBER 29 _____

The Benediction of Poverty

Looking at his disciples, he said: "Blessed are you who are poor, for yours is the kingdom of God" *(Luke 6:20)*.

T oday we are so afraid of poverty that we never dream of doing anything that might involve us in being poor. We are out of the running of medieval monks who took on the vow of poverty. Many of us are poor, but none of us chooses to be. Our attitude is that if we are extravagant a rainy day will come for which we have not laid up. You cannot lay up for a rainy day and justify it in the light of Jesus Christ's teaching.

The Treasures of Darkness

"I will give you the treasures of darkness, riches stored in secret places, so that you may know that I am the LORD, the God of Israel, who calls you by name" *(Isaiah 45:3).*

We often state the character of God in terms of brutal harshness which makes men atheists, while our motive is to glorify Him. Ever remember that "eternal life" is to know God; therefore you cannot expect to know Him in five minutes or forty years. Measure your ultimate delight in God's truth and joy in God by the little bit that is clear to you. There are whole tracts of God's character unrevealed to us as yet, and we have to bow in patience until God is able to reveal the things which look so dark. The danger is lest we make the little bit of truth we do know a pinnacle on which we set ourselves to judge everyone else.

The Shadow of God's Hand

"Though he slay me, yet will I hope in him; I will surely defend my ways to his face. Indeed, this might turn out for my deliverance, for no godless man would dare come before him!" *(Job 13:15–16).*

One of the saddest sights is to see Christians who were true go under through the lassitude of some sorrow. This is where it begins—God brought them under the shadow of His hand, and they said, "This is the devil, I have no business to be in darkness," forgetting that there are things God cannot explain. Our Lord taught over and

226

over again that things will never be explained in this life. We have to get rid of the idea that we are going to be vindicated down here; Jesus was not. The millennium age will be the vindication of the saints; this is the age of their humiliation.

NOVEMBER 1 _____

The Divine Drawing Power

Brothers, I do not consider myself yet to have taken hold of it. But one thing I do: Forgetting what is behind and straining toward what is ahead, I press on toward the goal to win the prize for which God has called me heavenward in Christ Jesus *(Philippians 3:13–14)*.

The Calling of God means that by receiving the nature of God I am called to the goal of God Himself. A man only hears the call of a thing if he has the nature of the thing within him, and then only if he broods on it. When I am born again the nature of God is put into me and whenever God is presented I feel the draw; I cannot get away from it. "I press on," says St. Paul, "if so be that I may apprehend that for which also I was apprehended by Christ Jesus." God saves a man apart from his own working; salvation is God's "bit" in every particular; what he has to do is to *work out* his own salvation.

NOVEMBER 2 _____

The Cost of Spiritual Perfection

"Be perfect, therefore, as your heavenly Father is perfect" *(Matthew 5:48)*.

I f I want to see the Face of God I must fast from other
things and concentrate on God. If in my inner life I
am under apprehension by Jesus Christ for the time being I
am out of touch with ordinary things. To fast is not to give
up food, but to cut off the right arm, and pluck out the right
eye. But that is only a stage; what we are tending towards is
the perfection Jesus speaks of in Matthew 5:48—"Ye
therefore shall be perfect, as your heavenly Father is
perfect"; but in order to get there we have to go the longest
way round. The end is a relationship to God perfect and
complete in every particular.

NOVEMBER 3 _____

Joy in True Devotion

"But we have this treasure in jars of clay to show that this
all-surpassing power is from God and not from us. We
are hard pressed on every side, but not crushed;
perplexed, but not in despair; persecuted, but not
abandoned; struck down, but not destroyed. We always
carry around in our body the death of Jesus, so that the
life of Jesus may also be revealed in our body. For we
who are alive are always being given over to death for
Jesus' sake, so that his life may be revealed in our mortal
body. So then, death is at work in us, but life is at work in
you. It is written: "I believed; therefore I have spoken."
With that same spirit of faith we also believe and
therefore speak, because we know that the one who
raised the Lord Jesus from the dead will also raise us
with Jesus and present us with you in his presence. All
this is for your benefit, so that the grace that is reaching
more and more people may cause thanksgiving to
overflow to the glory of God. Therefore we do not lose

heart. Though outwardly we are wasting away, yet inwardly we are being renewed day by day. For our light and momentary troubles are achieving for us an eternal glory that far outweighs them all. So we fix our eyes not on what is seen, but on what is unseen. for what is seen is temporary, but what is unseen is eternal" *(2 Corinthians 4:7–18))*.

C hristianity is not devotion to work, or to a cause, or a doctrine, but devotion to a Person, the Lord Jesus Christ. Christianity is a personal relationship which works spontaneously by "the moral originality of the Holy Ghost"; there is a perfect gaiety of delight. You could never awaken self-pity in the apostle Paul; you might starve him or imprison him, but you could never knock out of him that uncrushable gaiety and certainty of God. Paul refused to take anything or anyone seriously but Jesus Christ.

NOVEMBER 4 _____

Spiritual Detachment

What is more, I consider everything a loss compared to the surpassing greatness of knowing Christ Jesus my Lord, for whose sake I have lost all things. I consider them rubbish, that I may gain Christ *(Philippians 3:8)*.

G ive up your right to yourself to Me," says Jesus, "let Me realize Myself in you." He quenches the fury of desire by detaching us from things so that we may know Him. In this way God brings us into the fullness of life. The majority of us are not in the place where God can give us "the hundredfold more." We say, "A bird in the hand is worth two in the bush," while God is wanting to give us the bush with all the birds in it! It is necessary to be detached from things and then come back to them in a right relationship. A sense of property is a hindrance to spiritual growth; that is why so many of us know nothing about communion with Jesus Christ.

The Blessing of Affliction

Before I was afflicted I went astray, but now I obey your word *(Psalm 119:67)*.

I t is a terrible truth that many of us go astray until we are afflicted (see Psalm 119:67); we conceive in our pride that "we shall not be moved," and in this stage we dislike and radically disagree with the sterner presentations of God in the Bible, and it is only by the sharp sword of affliction and the profound conviction of the meanness of our pride that we are brought to see God for ourselves and are ready to turn and obey His commands.

The Danger of Disillusionment

So then, no more boasting about men! All things are yours *(1 Corinthians 3:21)*.

I n spiritual life disillusionment generally comes in relation to other people; that is why Paul says, "Wherefore let no one glory in men" (1 Corinthians 3:21) and ". . . not to think of himself more highly than he ought to think" (Romans 12:3). In Ezekiel 12 the disillusionment comes in connection with national life and is in relation to

God: the people begin to realize that God is not what they had vainly hoped He was. Verses 1–6 form God's answer to their expectation that He would reinstate the permanence of Jerusalem.

NOVEMBER 7

God's Secrets Revealed in the Dark

"The secret things belong to the LORD our God, but the things revealed belong to us and to our children forever, that we may follow all the words of this law" *(Deuteronomy 29:29)*.

There are depths inaccessible in the Divine nature; mysteries unrevealed in the method of God's procedure. God never reveals anything ahead of moral and spiritual progress. The Christian worker who has never walked in the darkness of God's hand with no light, has never walked with God at all. The principle of walking with God is that it is a walk by faith, not by sight; a walk in the light of Christ, not in the light of dogmatic conviction. Jesus as our example was under the shadow of the hand of God. "If it is possible, let this cup pass from Me."

NOVEMBER 8

The Freedom of the Father's Child

"And do not call anyone on earth 'father,' for you have one Father, and he is in heaven" *(Matthew 23:9)*.

George MacDonald in one of his books gives a graphic description of the wonderful simplicity a child of God

231

has; he pictures Job opening God's private door, as it were, and flinging himself into His presence and presenting his problems. He is indicating the freedom a child of God has to come and say, "I am puzzled by this and that; why should things be so?" He is coming not to a monarch who will terrify him, but to a Father, if he is a disciple, and he can speak just like a child with perfect simplicity and freedom. Some of us seem to have the idea that we are away in a howling wilderness and we must cry and agonize before we can get God's ear. Turn to the New Testament and see what Jesus says—"Father, I thank Thee that Thou hast heard Me. And I knew that Thou hearest Me always."

NOVEMBER 9 _____

The Supreme Teacher

> "But the Counselor, the Holy Spirit, whom the Father will send in my name, will teach you all things and will remind you of everything I have said to you" *(John 14:26).*

The test of every spiritual impulse is, does it make Jesus Christ the supreme Teacher? Jesus said, "When the Holy Spirit is come, He shall teach you all things." The Holy Spirit is the great bond of union because He keeps us united to the one Teacher. Jesus Christ is not a great Teacher alongside Plato and other great teachers; He stands absolutely alone. "Test your teachers," said Jesus; the teachers who come from God are those who clear the way to Jesus Christ, and keep it clear. We are estimated in God's sight as workers by whether or not we clear the way for people to see Jesus.

The Blameworthy Temper

"Save me, O LORD, from lying lips and from deceitful tongues. What will he do to you, and what more besides, O deceitful tongue? He will punish you with a warrior's sharp arrows, with burning coals of the broom tree" *(Psalm 120:2–4).*

The suffering which springs from being "a meddler in other men's matters" (a busybody) is humiliating to the last degree. A free translation of 1 Thessalonians 4:11 might well read: "Study to shut up and mind your own business"; and among all the texts we hang on our walls, let this be one. The suffering that arises from a wrong temper has no refining side, but only a humiliating one. "Therefore take heed to your spirit." A blameworthy temper of mind is the most damning thing in the human soul.

The Altar of Sacrifice

But even if I am being poured out like a drink offering on the sacrifice and service coming from your faith, I am glad and rejoice with all of you *(Philippians 2:17).*

Paul's conception of the altar of sacrifice is "spending and being spent" for the sake of the elementary children of God. He has no other end and aim than that— to be broken bread and poured-out wine in the hands of God that others might be nourished and fed (cf. Colossians 1:24). The great Saviour and His great apostle go hand-in-hand—the Son of God sacrificed Himself that men might be redeemed; Paul, the bondslave of Jesus, sacrifices himself that men might accept the Great Salvation.

The Mind of Christ

Your attitude should be the same as that of Christ Jesus *(Philippians 2:5)*.

When we are born again we are not given a fully formed reasoning Christian mind; we are given the Spirit of Jesus, but not His mind; we have to form that. Countless numbers of men and women are saved who never think of forming the mind of Christ. The "mind" Paul urges these Philippian Christians to form is not the mind of Almighty God, but "the mind of Christ Jesus, who esteemed His own identity with God not a thing to be grasped at." This was the central citadel of the temptation—"You are the Son of God, then assert Your prerogative; You can bring the world to Your feet if You will only remember who You are and use Your power." The invariable answer Jesus made was, "I came not to do Mine own will though I am the Son of God; I am here in this order of things for one purpose only, to do the will of My Father."

Where and How to Shine

So that you may become blameless and pure, children of God without fault in a crooked and depraved generation, in which you shine like stars in the universe *(Philippians 2:15)*.

We have to shine as lights in the squalid places of earth; we can't shine in heaven; our light would be put out in two seconds. If ever we are to be blameless, undeserving of censure in the sight of God who sees down to the motives of our motives, it must be by the supernatural power of God. That is the meaning of the Cross, that through it I can not only have God's marvelous work done in my heart, but I can have the proof of it in my life.

NOVEMBER 14 _____

Are We Profaning His Holy Name?

"And wherever they went among the nations they profaned my holy name, for it was said of them, 'These are the LORD'S people, and yet they had to leave his land' " *(Ezekiel 36:20)*.

This was the characteristic of the people of God whenever they forgot whose they were and whom they served. Under the searchlight of God we realize that God's holy Name is profaned when we put before people what God's grace has wrought in us instead of God Himself. Whenever we go into work for God from any standpoint saving that of the dominance of God, we begin to patronize at once; unless we go as the bondservants of Jesus Christ we have no business to go at all. Jesus Christ became the towel-girt Servant of His own disciples. Never deal with people from the superior person's standpoint, God never blesses that; deal only by steadily presenting the Lord Jesus Christ. The characteristic of the holiness which is the outcome of the indwelling of God is a blazing truthfulness with regard to God's Word, and an amazing tenderness in personal dealing.

Happiness, a False Goal

This is what the wicked are like—always carefree, they increase in wealth *(Psalm 73:12)*.

" 'And I'll say to myself, "You have plenty of good things laid up for many years. Take life easy; eat, drink, and be merry" ' *(Luke 12:19)*.

H appiness is the portion of a child; a child ought to be thoughtless and happy, and woe be to the people who upset their happiness. But if you take happiness as the end and aim for men and women, you have to make its basis a determined ignorance of God; otherwise men will, like Job, "remember God and be troubled" (Job 23:15). Read the seventy-third Psalm; it is the description of the man who has made happiness his aim—he is not in trouble as other men, neither is he plagued like other men; he has more than heart could wish; but once let his moral equilibrium be upset by conviction of sin and all his happiness is destroyed. The coming of Jesus Christ is not a peaceful thing, but a disturbing thing, because it means the destruction of every happiness that is not based on a personal relationship to Himself.

God's Method: The Corn of Wheat

"I tell you the truth, unless a kernel of wheat falls to the ground and dies, it remains only a single seed. But if it dies, it produces many seeds" *(John 12:24).*

T his fundamental principle must ever be borne in mind—that any work for God, before it fulfills its purpose, must die, otherwise it abides alone. Outside the Bible, the conception is of progressing from a seed to full growth; in the Bible the conception is of a seed corrupting itself into what it never was. Watch the history of any spiritual work; you will find it begins magnificently and then fizzles out, and if you are not in the secret, you will say, "What a discouraging business!" The devil would conserve it into a little crystallized compartment and make us worship it, but God sends His forces and disintegrates it into the same kind of failure that the life of His Son was, and then He brings out in fruit something no man ever dreamt of. Christianity is always a forlorn hope in the eyes of the world; it is always dying and bringing forth what it never was.

The Fortune of Misfortune

Now I want you to know, brothers, that what has happened to me has really served to advance the gospel *(Philippians 1:12).*

T he fortune of misfortune! That is Paul's way of looking at his captivity. He does not want them to be depressed on his account, or to imagine that God's purposes have been hindered; he says they have not been hindered, but furthered. The very things which looked so disastrous have turned out to be the most opportune, so that on this account the apostle's heart is bounding with joy, and the same note of rejoicing is found throughout the whole Letter.

NOVEMBER 18 _____

Instruments or Servants

It is true that some preach Christ out of envy and rivalry, but others out of good will *(Philippians 1:15)*.

An instrument of God and a servant of God ought to be identical, but our Lord's words in Matthew 7 and Paul's words here are instances where they are not. It does not impair the inspiration of the Gospel to have it preached by a bad man, but the influence of the preacher, worthy or unworthy, apart altogether from his preaching, has a tremendous effect. If I know a man to be a bad man, the sinister influence of his personality neutralizes altogether the effect of God's message through him to me; but let me be sure that my intuition springs from my own relationship to God and not from human suspicion.

NOVEMBER 19 _____

Holiness Imparted

And be found in him, not having a righteousness of my own that comes from the law, but that which is through faith in Christ—the righteousness that comes from God and is by faith *(Philippians 3:9)*.

The only holiness there is, is the holiness derived through faith, and faith is the instrument the Holy Spirit uses to organize us into Christ. But do not let us be vague here. Holiness, like sin, is not a series of acts; it is a disposition. A man can act holily, but he has not a holy *disposition.* A saint has had imparted to him the disposition of holiness; there holiness is to be the characteristic of the life here and now. Entire sanctification is the end of the disposition of sin, but only the beginning of the life of the saint, then comes growth in holiness. The process of sanctification begins at the moment of birth from above, and is consummated on the unconditional surrender of my right to myself to Jesus Christ. The time that elapses between new birth and entire sanctification depends entirely on the individual.

NOVEMBER 20 _____

God Can Undo the Past

"I will repay you for the years the locusts have eaten—
the great locust and the young locust, the other locusts
and the locust swarm—my great army that I sent among
you" *(Joel 2:25).*

In a crisis leave everything to God; shut out every voice saving the voice of God and the psalm of your own deliverance; make it your duty to remain true to both these voices.

In the life of a saint tribulation does this supernatural thing—it brings back innocence with experience; in the natural world experience brings cunning and craftiness. We sit down under the tyranny of a devil's lie and say, "I can't undo the past"; you cannot, but God can. God can make the past, as far as our spiritual life is concerned, as if it had never been and even in its worst features He can make it bring out the "treasures of darkness."

"Jacob Was Left Alone"

So Jacob was left alone, and a man wrestled with him till daybreak *(Genesis 32:24)*.

A nd Jacob was left alone" (v. 24).

This phrase is significant because in his loneliness Jacob goes through the decisive struggle of his life. We are dealing in this chapter with Jacob the giant, not with the mean man. ". . . and there wrestled a man with him until the breaking of the day." Jacob tried to strangle the answer to his own prayer; his wrestling represents the human fighting with God. The noblest ones in God's sight are those who do not struggle but go through without demur. Abraham did not wrestle, neither did Isaac; Jacob struggles for everything. If a man has difficulty in getting through to God we are apt to imagine it is an indication of a fine character whereas the opposite is true; he is refusing to yield and is kicking, and the only thing God can do is to cripple him. The characteristics exhibited by Jacob are those of Peter before Pentecost and Saul of Tarsus before his conversion, a mixture of the dastardly and the heroic, the mean and the noble, all jumbled up.

"Jacob Halted on His Thigh"

The sun rose above him as he passed Peniel, and he was
limping because of his hip *(Genesis 32:31)*.

J acob's wrestling means that he did not want to go
through the way he knew he must; he had to come to
the end of the best of his natural self, to go to the "white
funeral" of his own wisdom, and he struggled in order not
to. Then he came to the place where his wisdom was
crippled forever. "And he halted upon his thigh." The
symbol is expressive of what it looks like in the eyes of
shrewd worldly wisdom to cast yourself unperplexed on
God. When we cling to God we learn to kneel for the first
time.

If you have never been to "Peniel" you are sure to come
across things that will put your human wisdom into a panic;
if you have seen God face to face your circumstances will
never arouse any panic in you. We run off at a tangent—
anywhere but Peniel where we would see God face to face.

Spirit, Soul, and Body

May God himself, the God of peace, sanctify you
through and through. May your whole spirit, soul and
body be kept blameless at the coming of our Lord Jesus
Christ *(1 Thessalonians 5:23)*.

S oul is the rational expression of my personal spirit in
my body, the way I reason and think and work.
Habits are formed in the soul, not in the spirit, and they are

formed in the soul by means of the body. Jesus Christ told His disciples that they must lose their soul, i.e., their way of reasoning and looking at things, and begin to estimate from an entirely different standpoint. For a while a born-again soul is inarticulate, it has no expression; the equilibrium has been upset by the incoming of a totally new spirit into the human spirit, and the reasoning faculties are disturbed. "In your patience possess ye your souls," says Jesus; i.e., the new way of looking at things must be acquired with patience. On the basis of His Redemption Jesus Christ claims that He can put into my personal spirit His own heredity, viz., Holy Spirit; then I have to form character on the basis of that new disposition. God will do everything I cannot do, but He will do nothing He has constructed me to do.

NOVEMBER 24

The Cleansing of the Unconscious

Who can discern his errors? Forgive my hidden faults. Keep your servant also from willful sins; may they not rule over me. Then will I be blameless, innocent of great transgression *(Psalm 19:12–12)*.

But if we walk in the light, as he is in the light, we have fellowship with one another, and the blood of Jesus. his Son, purifies us from all sin *(1 John 1:7)*.

C leansing from all sin does not mean conscious deliverance from sin only; it means infinitely more than we are conscious of. The part we are conscious of is walking in the light: cleansing from all sin means something infinitely profounder; it means cleansing from all sin in the sight of God. God never bases any of His work on our consciousness. "Do you mean to tell me that God can search me to the inmost recesses of my dreams, my inmost motives, and find nothing to blame? That God Almighty can bring the winnowing fan of His Spirit and search out my thoughts and imaginations, and find nothing to blame?" Who can stand before God and say, My hands are clean, my heart is pure? Who can climb that hill of the Lord? No man under heaven, saving the man who has been readjusted at the Cross of Christ.

NOVEMBER 25

The Transforming Power of Regeneration

Because our gospel came to you not simply with words, but also with power, with the Holy Spirit and with deep conviction you know how we lived among you for your sake (1 Thessalonians 1:5).

I f our body has been the slave of wrong habits physically, mentally, and morally, we must get hold of a power big enough to remake our habits, and that power lies in the word *Regeneration*. "If any man be in Christ, he is a new creature"; that means this marvelous thing—that I may be loosened from every wrong habit I have formed if only I will obey the Spirit of God. Immediately I do obey, I find I can begin to form new habits in accordance with His commands, and prove physically, mentally and morally that I am a new creation. That is why it is so necessary to receive the Holy Spirit; then when God gives a command it is sufficient to know He has told me to do it and I find I can do it. Frequently God has to say to us—"Say no more to Me

243

on this matter; don't everlastingly cry to Me about this thing, do it yourself, keep your forces together and go forward." God is for you, the Spirit of God is in you, and every place that the sole of your foot shall tread upon, shall be yours.

NOVEMBER 26 _____

The Secret of Radiance

> For it is light that makes everything visible. This is why it is said: "Wake up, O sleeper, rise from the dead, and Christ will shine on you" *(Ephesians 5:14).*

The joy that Jesus gives is the result of our disposition being at one with His own disposition. The Spirit of God will fill us to overflowing if we will be careful to keep in the light. We have no business to be weak in God's strength.

"Look therefore carefully how ye walk." We have to walk in the light "as He is in the light"; keep continually coming to the light; don't keep anything covered up. If we are filled with the life of Jesus we must walk circumspectly, keep the interest in life going, have nothing folded up. The evidence that we are being filled with the life of God is that we are not deceived about the things that spring from ourselves and the things that spring from Jesus Christ. "If you have sinned," says John, "confess it, keep in the light all through."

God Gives the Body: We Form the Habits

Therefore, when Christ came into the world, he said: "Sacrifice and offering you did not desire, but a body you prepared for me" *(Hebrews 10:5).*

And whatever you do, whether in word or deed, do it all in the name of the Lord Jesus, giving thanks to God the Father through him *(Colossians 3:17).*

T he difference between a sentimental Christian and a sanctified saint is just here. The sanctified saint is one who has disciplined the body into perfect obedience to the dictates of the Spirit of God; consequently his body does with the greatest of ease whatever God wants him to do. The sentimental type of Christian is the sighing, tear-flowing, beginning-over-again Christian who always has to go to prayer meetings, always has to be stirred up, or to be soothed and put in bandages, because he has never formed the habit of obedience to the Spirit of God. Our spiritual life does not grow *in spite of* the body, but *because* of the body.

Christ, the Context of Scripture

"You diligently study the Scriptures because you think that by them you possess eternal life. These are the Scriptures that testify about me, yet you refuse to come to me to have life" *(John 5:39–40).*

T hese verses reveal how a knowledge of the Scriptures may distort the mind away from Jesus Christ. Unless

245

we know the Living Word personally first, the literal words may lead us astray. The only way we can understand the Bible is by personal contact with the Living Word; then the Holy Spirit expounds the literal words to us along the line of personal experience. "The words I speak unto you, they are spirit and they are life." The Jews knew the Scriptures thoroughly, yet their minds were so distorted that when they saw Jesus Christ they said, "He hath a devil." There is a context to the Bible, and Jesus Christ is that Context. The right order is personal relationship to Him first, then the interpretation of the Scriptures according to His Spirit.

NOVEMBER 29

The Peril of Unfulfilled Vows

> Do not be quick with your mouth, do not be hasty in your heart to utter anything before God. God is in heaven and you are on earth, so let your words be few (*Ecclesiastes 5:2*).

T o make a promise may simply be a way of shirking responsibility. Never pile up promises before men, and certainly not before God. It is better to run the risk of being considered indecisive, better to be uncertain and not promise, than to promise and not fulfill. "Better is it that thou shouldest not vow, than that thou shouldest vow and not pay."

The vices of vowing outweigh the virtues, because vowing is built on a misconception of human nature as it really is. If a man had the power to will pure will, it would be different, but he has not. There are certain things a man cannot do, not because he is bad, but because he is not constituted to do them. We make vows which are impossible of fulfillment because no man can remain master of himself always; there comes a time when the human will must yield allegiance to a force greater than itself; it must yield either to God or to the devil.

NOVEMBER 30 _____

The Ultimate Witness—"Unto Me"

"But you will receive power when the Holy Spirit comes on you; and you will be my witnesses in Jerusalem, and in all Judea and Samaria, and to the ends of the earth" (Acts 1:8).

When we are born again of the Spirit the note of our testimony is what God has done for us, and rightly so; but the baptism of the Holy Ghost obliterates that forever. God will never answer our prayer to be baptized by the Holy Ghost for any other reason than to be a witness for Jesus. "Ye shall receive power, after that the Holy Ghost is come upon you: and ye shall be witnesses unto Me. . . ." Not witnesses of what Jesus can do, that is an elementary witness, but "witnesses unto Me"—you will be instead of Me, you will take everything that happens, praise or blame, persecution or commendation, as happening to Me. No one can stand that unless he is constrained by the majesty of the personal power of Jesus. Paul says I am constrained by the love of Christ, held as in a fever, gripped as by a disease, that is why I act as I do; you may call me mad or sober, I do not care; I am after only one thing—to persuade men of the judgment seat of Christ and of the love of God.

247

Walking in God's Light

But if we walk in the light, as he is in the light, we have
fellowship with one another, and the blood of Jesus, his
Son, purifies us from all sin *(1 John 1:7).*

A born-again soul is condemned to holiness; he is not at
liberty to do what he likes but only what God likes, a
"bondslave of Jesus"; my relationship to God first, second,
and third and all the time. The modern note is that we have
sinned against this one and that one: every sin we commit
against another is a sin against God, and the Bible brings us
face to face with God. Can my salvation stand the glaring
light of God? Can my relationship with my fellow men
stand the light of God? It has got to one day. That is the
way the Spirit of God rouses us up to see that there is no
refuge in anything or anyone other than Himself. The
whole life must be established in God. The one thing that
keeps us right is walking in the light of the great High God.

Search Me, O God

Search me, O God, and know my heart; test me and
know my anxious thoughts *(Psalms 139:23).*

We make mistakes through not knowing the way we are
designed. For instance, people talk about inattention
as if it came from the devil, whereas it really arises from a
complete misunderstanding of the way we are made. Psalm
139 is a psalm of introspective intercession; the Psalmist
realizes that he is a great deal more than he can grasp; there

are deeper depths in him and higher heights than in the sea or the mountains; but he does not leave himself in abstractions; he comes straight back to God, "Search me, O God, and know my heart."

DECEMBER 3 _____

Disposition and Character

> Therefore, my dear friends, as you have always obeyed—not only in my presence, but now much more in my absence—continue to work out your salvation with fear and trembling *(Philippians 2:12)*.

A man must make his own character, but he cannot make his disposition. Naturally our disposition is gifted to us by heredity, and in Regeneration God gives to us the disposition of His Son. Neither when we are born into this world nor when we are born again are we given character: character is the thing we must make, and it works in the same way when we are spiritual as when we are natural. You cannot estimate a man's character by isolated things, but only by the main trend of the life. Character represents the difference between disposition and the working of it out actually.

DECEMBER 4 _____

From the Old to the New

> Therefore, if anyone is in Christ, he is a new creation; the old has gone, the new has come! *(2 Corinthians 5:17)*.

The Bible reveals that the natural virtues are remnants of what the human race was as God designed it, i.e., the natural virtues belong to an order that is no longer appearing. The "man of old" has to pass and the "new man" has to dominate, but in the meantime there is chaos. The great thing to realize is that our physical nature is the same after we are born again as we were before; the difference is in the ruling disposition.

DECEMBER 5

God and My Character

To the faithful you show yourself faithful, to the blameless you show yourself blameless, to the pure you show yourself pure, but to the crooked you show yourself shrewd *(Psalm 18:25–26).*

T he revelation of God to me is determined by the state of my character toward God. "With the merciful Thou wilt shew Thyself merciful;" says the Psalmist, "and with the perverse Thou wilt shew Thyself froward." If we persist in being stiff-necked toward God, we will find He is stiff-necked toward us; if we show ourselves meek toward God, He will reveal Himself as gentle toward us.

DECEMBER 6

The Danger of Disloyalty

Whom have I in heaven but you? And being with you, I desire nothing on earth. My flesh and my heart may fail, but God is the strength of my heart and my portion forever. Those who are far from you will perish; you destroy all who are unfaithful to you. But as for me, it is good to be near God. I have made the Sovereign LORD my refuge; I will tell of all your deeds" *(Psalm 73:25–28)*.

N one of us is free from disloyalty unless we are absolutely loyal. We are always on the wrong line when we come to God with a preoccupied mind, because a preoccupied mind springs from a disloyal heart: "I don't want to do God's will; what I want is for God to give me permission to do what I want to do." That is disloyalty, and the experience of Psalm 106:15 is the inevitable result— "And He gave them their request; but sent leanness into their soul."

DECEMBER 7 _____

At The Foot of Jacob's Ladder

He then added, "I tell you the truth, you shall see heaven open, and the angels of God ascending and descending on the Son of Man" *(John 1:51)*.

J acob is the man who represents life as it is. The world is not made up of saints or of devils, but of people like you and like me, and our real home is at the foot of Jacob's ladder with the sneak. Never say that God intended a man to have a domain of dreaming mighty visions of God, and at the same time be dead towards God in his actual life. Jesus Christ claims that He can make the real and the actual one, as they were in His own life.

DECEMBER 8 _____

The Road Back to Yesterday

> "I will repay you for the years the locusts have eaten—
> the great locust and the young locust, the other locusts
> and the locust swarm—my great army that I sent among
> you" *(Joel 2:25)*.

T hrough the Redemption God undertakes to deal with
a man's past, and He does it in two ways: by forgiving
him, and by making the past a wonderful culture for the
future. The forgiveness of God is a bigger miracle than we
are apt to think. It is impossible for a human being to
forgive; and it is because this is not realized that we fail to
understand that the forgiveness of God is a miracle of
Divine grace. Do I really believe that God cannot, dare not,
must not forgive me my sin without its being atoned for? If
God were to forgive me my sin without its being atoned for,
I should have a greater sense of justice than God. It is not
that God says in effect, "I will pay no more attention to
what you have done." When God forgives a man, He not
only alters him but transmutes what he has already done.

DECEMBER 9 _____

The Divine Paradox, Solved in the Incarnation

> Then I saw a Lamb, looking as if it had been slain,
> standing in the center of the throne, encircled by the four
> living creatures and the elders. He had seven horns and
> seven eyes, which are the seven spirits of God sent out
> into all the earth *(Revelation 5:6)*.

beheld a Lamb!" In the book of Isaiah a paradox of a similar nature occurs; the prophet has been looking for some great conquering army of the Lord and instead he sees a lonely Figure, "travelling in the greatness of his strength," and he asks "Who is this that cometh from Edom?" If you take all the manifestations of God given in the Old Testament you find them a mass of contradiction— now God is pictured as a Man, now as a Woman, now as a lonely Hero, now as a suffering Servant, and until we come to the New Testament these conflicting characteristics but add confusion to our conception of God. But immediately we see Jesus Christ, we find all the apparent contradictions blended in one unique Personality.

DECEMBER 10 _____

Tempted in All Points

> For we do not have a high priest who is unable to sympathize with our weaknesses, but we have one who has been tempted in every way, just as we are—yet was without sin (Hebrews 4:15).

Jesus Christ took on Him our physical frailty, not our moral frailty—that would mean He had moral perversity on the inside; and in this physical frame He lived a spotlessly holy life. If Jesus Christ had not partaken of our human frailty He could never have been tempted; it would have been a pretence; but He is not tempted "in all points like as we are" before we have been made "His brethren" by sanctification (see 2:11). Every temptation possible to us after that experience, He knows all about, and we can be more than conquerors through Him.

The Way Prepared, the Glory Revealed

A voice of one calling: "In the desert prepare the way for the LORD, make straight in the wilderness a highway for our God. Every valley shall be raised up, every mountain and hill made low; the rough ground shall become level, the rugged places a plain. And the glory of the LORD will be revealed, and all mankind together will see it. For the mouth of the LORD has spoken" *(Isaiah 40:3–5).*

U nless we prepare on the outside in accordance with the inner vision we are not in God's order. John the Baptist prepared the way of the Lord historically, but take it personally—how many valleys have I exalted, and how many mountains have I made low? How many mountains of prejudice have I put out of the way? If we prepare on the outside we enable God to plant His glory there, and the first thing we have to do is to go dead against our ingrained prejudices which put a barrier round about us. If I will *do* in accordance with what God has made me *be,* He will reveal His glory.

The Blessing of the Pure in Heart

Blessed are the pure in heart, for they will see God *(Matthew 5:8).*

T he vision of God's purpose comes from a pure heart, from acute intellect; the condition is—the inner life right with God. An illiterate old woman with a pure heart has a greater insight into the purposes of God than a prime minister. If the prime minister has a pure heart as well as powerful intellect, then you have a man like Isaiah, a giant for God. The sanctification-metaphysic underlies everything. The opportunity is given to us all to be the choice souls. The God who guides the stars, unhasting and unresting, will as assuredly fulfill what He has promised.

DECEMBER 13

God's Message to a Disobedient People

Comfort, comfort my people, says your God. Speak tenderly to Jerusalem, and proclaim to her that her hard service has been completed, that her sin has been paid for, that she has received from the LORD's hand double for all her sins *((Isaiah 40:1–2)*.

"C omfort ye, comfort ye My people, saith your God." Notice the "My," and remember that they were a disobedient people, and yet God is "not ashamed to be called their God." It is not the love of God for a pure saint, but the love of God for a sin-stained people. He might well have been ashamed of them on account of their sin and degradation, but His voice comes in all its amazing wonder—"Speak ye comfortably" ("to the heart of," R.V. marg.) "to Jerusalem, . . ." It is a wonderful picture of what God does in the Atonement.

DECEMBER 14

Help From on High

He reached down from on high and took hold of me; he drew me out of deep waters *(Psalm 18:16)*.

255

And God raised us up with Christ and seated us with him
in the heavenly realms in Christ Jesus *(Ephesians 2:6)*.

T he Lord Jesus Christ is the Highest; is there anyone
higher to you? Your life is never safeguarded until
Jesus is seen to be the Highest. Past experience will not
keep you, neither will deliverance from sin; the only
safeguarding power is the Highest. If there is a breath of
confidence anywhere else there will be disaster, and it is by
the mercy of God that you are allowed to stumble or be
pain-smitten, until you learn that He does it all—*He* keeps
you from stumbling. *He* raises you up and keeps you. *He*
sends from above and delivers you.

DECEMBER 15 _____

Gracious Manifestation of the Life of God

Isaac planted crops in that land and the same year
reaped a hundredfold, because the LORD blessed him.
The man became rich, and his wealth continued to grow
until he became very wealthy. He had so many flocks
and herds and servants that the Philistines envied him.
So all the wells that his father's servants had dug in the
time of his father Abraham, the Philistines stopped up,
filling them with earth. Then Abimelech said to Isaac,
"Move away from us; you have become too powerful for
us." So Isaac moved away from there and encamped in
the Valley of Gerar and settled there. Isaac reopened the
wells that had been dug in the time of his father
Abraham, which the Philistines had stopped up after
Abraham died, and he gave them the same names his
father had given them. Isaac's servants dug in the valley
and discovered a well of fresh water there. But the
herdsmen of Gerar quarreled with Isaac's herdsmen and

said, "The water is ours!" So he named the well Esek, because they disputed with him. Then they dug another well, but they quarreled over that one also; so he named it Sitnah. He moved on from there and dug another well, and no one quarreled over it. He named it Rehoboth, saying, "Now the LORD has given us room and we will flourish in the land *(Genesis 26:12–22).*

T he only right a Christian has is the right to give up his rights. This is the tender grace which is usually looked upon as an exhibition of lack of gumption. The embarrassing thing about Christian graces is that immediately you imitate them they become nauseating, because conscious imitation implies an affected preference for certain qualities, and we produce frauds by a spurious piety. To have the attitudes of life without the life itself is a fraud; to have the life itself imitating the best Pattern of that life is normal and right (see 1 Peter 2:21–23). All the qualities of godly life are characteristic of the life of God; you cannot imitate the life of God unless you have it, and then the imitation is not conscious, but the unconscious manifestation of the real thing.

DECEMBER 16 _____

Concentration on the Highest

Who among you fears the LORD and obeys the word of his servant? Let him who walks in the dark, who has no light, trust in the name of the LORD and rely on his God *(Isaiah 50:10).*

W henever there is a complication in your circumstances do nothing until you see the Highest, not sometimes, but always (cf. Isaiah 50:10). Can you see the Lord in your thinking? If not, suspend your judgment until you can. Can you see the face of Jesus in your affections? If not, restrain them until you can. Can you see God in your circumstances? If not, do nothing until you can. Our Lord can trust anything to the man or woman who has seen Him.

"Set your affection on things above," says Paul; gather in the stray impulses and fix them. The spiritual life is not impulsive; we are impulsive when we are not spiritual. In every experience the standard is our Lord Himself, and He was never impulsive; impulse was the one thing He always checked. Impulse has to be trained and turned into intuition by discipline.

DECEMBER 17 _____

"Whatsoever Things Are Lovely"

> Finally, brothers, whatever is true, whatever is noble, whatever is right, whatever is pure, whatever is lovely, whatever is admirable—if anything is excellent or praiseworthy—think about such things *(Philippians 4:8)*.

The word *lovely* has the meaning of juicy and delicious. We have the idea that our duty must always be disagreeable, and we make any number of duties out of diseased sensibilities. If our duty is disagreeable, it is a sign that we are in a disjointed relationship to God. If God gave some people a fully sweet cup, they would go carefully into a churchyard and turn the cup upside down and empty it, and say, "No, that could never be meant for me." Duty is the daughter of God. Never take your estimate of duty after a sleepless night, or after a dose of indigestion; take your sense of duty from the Spirit of God and the word of Jesus.

There are people whose lives are diseased and twisted by a sense of duty which God never inspired; but once let them begin to think about the things of loveliness, and the healing forces that will come into their lives will be amazing. The very essence of godliness is in the things of loveliness; think about them, says Paul.

DECEMBER 18 ————————————————————————

"Things of Good Report"

Finally, brothers, whatever is true, whatever is noble, whatever is right, whatever is pure, whatever is lovely, whatever is admirable—if anything is excellent or praise-worthy—think about such things *(Philippians 4:8)*.

When we do think about the things of good report we shall be astonished to realize where they are to be found; they are found where we only expected to find the opposite. When our eyes are fixed on Jesus Christ we begin to see qualities blossoming in the lives of others that we never saw there before. We see people whom we have tabooed and put on the other side exhibiting qualities we have never exhibited, although we call ourselves saved and sanctified. Never look for other people to be holy; it is a cruel thing to do; it distorts your view of yourself and of others. Could anyone have had a sterner view of sin than Jesus had, and yet had anyone a more loving tender patience with the worst of men than He had? The difference in the attitude is that Jesus Christ never expected men to be holy; He knew they could not be: *He came to make men holy.* All He asks of men is that they acknowledge they are not right; then He will do all the rest.

DECEMBER 19

Joy Among the Unexpected

When the LORD brought back the captives to Zion, we were like men who dreamed. Our mouths were filled with laughter, our tongues with songs of joy. Then it was said among the nations, "The LORD has done great things for them." The LORD has done great things for us, and we are filled with joy. Restore our fortunes, O LORD, like streams in the Negev. Those who sow in tears will reap with songs of joy. He who goes out weeping, carrying seed to sow, will return with songs of joy, carrying sheaves with him" *(Psalm 126:1–6).*

T he characteristic of this passage is the unexpectedness of the happenings. "Then was our mouth filled with laughter, and our tongue with singing." We never dreamed that such a thing would happen to us! This attitude of mind frequently comes by the way of a calamity. Many a man has had his soul restored in the valley of the shadow, not in the green pastures. There are clouds we fear to enter, but on the inside of these clouds is the suddenness of real light. We get the evidence of this on the threshold of real sorrow and difficulty; there is the suddenness of real light and a discernment of things that was unsought, which we could get in no other way.

DECEMBER 20

A Second Adam, to the Rescue Came

The angel answered, "The Holy Spirit will come upon you, and the power of the Most High will overshadow

260

you. So the holy one to be born will be called the Son of God" *(Luke 1:35).*

T he Holy Ghost shall come upon thee, and the power of the Highest shall overshadow thee: therefore also that holy thing which shall be born of thee shall be called the Son of God."

The New Testament reveals that the birth of Jesus was an advent, not a beginning—an advent that put Him on the plane, humanly speaking, that Adam was on. The first Adam and the last Adam came direct from the hand of God.

God did not create Adam holy; He created him innocent, without self-consciousness (as we understand the word) before God; the one thing Adam was conscious of was God and only of himself in relation to the Being Whose commands he was to fill; the main trend of his spirit was towards God. Adam was intended by God to take part in his own development by a series of moral choices whereby he would transform innocence into holiness. Adam failed to do this. Jesus Christ came on the same platform as Adam and did not fail.

DECEMBER 21 _____

Son of God, Son of Man: The God-Man

In the beginning was the Word, and the Word was with God, and the Word was God. . . .

The Word became flesh and lived for a while among us. We have seen his glory, the glory of the one and only Son, who came from the Father, full of grace and truth. . . . V1 No one has ever seen God, but God the

261

only Son, who is at the Father's side, has made him known *(John 1:1, 14, 18)*.

T here are phases of the Life of Our Lord presented in the New Testament that no other life, so-called, deals with. If you start with the theory that Jesus Christ was a man who became God, you have to leave out any number of New Testament facts; if you say that Jesus Christ was God and His manhood a seeming phase, you have to miss out other facts. The Person of Jesus Christ revealed in the New Testament is unique—God-Man. In Him we deal with God as Man, the God-Man, the Representative of the whole human race in one Person. Jesus Christ is not a Being with two personalities; He is *Son of God* —the exact expression of Almighty God and *Son of Man*—the presentation of God's normal Man.

DECEMBER 22 _____

The Purpose of the Incarnation

"She will give birth to a son, and you are to give him the name Jesus, because he will save his people from their sins" *(Matthew 1:21)*.

J esus Christ became Incarnate for one purpose, to make a way back to God that man might stand before Him as he was created to do, the friend and lover of God Himself. The Atonement means infinitely more than we can conceive; it means that we can be morally identified with Jesus Christ until we understand what the apostle Paul meant when he said, "I live; yet not I, but Christ liveth in me." All the mighty efficacy of the Death of Jesus, of His Resurrection and Ascension to the right hand of the throne of God, is implanted into us by regeneration. And the lowest and most sin-stained can go that way. The measure of the salvation of Jesus is not that it does for the best man we know, but that it does for the worst and most sin-stained. There is no son of man that need despair; Jesus Christ can reproduce His saving work in any and every man, blessed be the Name of God!

DECEMBER 23

The Word Made Weak

The Word became flesh and lived for a while among us. We have seen his glory, the glory of the one and only Son, who came from the Father, full of grace and truth (John 1:14).

I f you look upon Jesus Christ from the commonsense standpoint you will never discern who He is; but if you look upon Him as God "manifested in the flesh" for the purpose of putting the whole human race back to where God designed it to be, you get the meaning of the Redemption. To the commonsense standpoint of His own day Jesus Christ was "the carpenter's son" (see Matthew 13:55). We do not deal with Jesus Christ as the Carpenter of Nazareth: we deal with the Carpenter of Nazareth as *God manifested in the flesh.*

DECEMBER 24

Why the Second Adam Came

But the gift is not like the trespass. For if the many died by the trespass of the one man, how much more did

God's grace and the gift that came by the grace of the one man, Jesus Christ, overflow to the many! *(Romans 5:15)*.

W hen Jesus Christ, the last Adam, came it was not men's external sins He aimed at, but something more fundamental, viz., the heredity of sin—my claim to my right to myself. The Redemption deals with the thing no man can deal with, his heredity. Apart from Jesus Christ I am always more than mastered by sin. ". . . sold under sin," says Paul.

"Him who knew no sin He made to be sin on our behalf"; The revelation is not that Jesus Christ was punished for our sins, but that He was *made to be sin*. The Son of God became the very thing which had severed man from God, and becoming it, He put it away.

DECEMBER 25 _____

'O, Come to My Heart Lord Jesus'

But when God, who set me apart from birth and called me by his grace, was pleased to reveal his Son in me so that I might preach him among the Gentiles, I did not consult any man, nor did I go up to Jerusalem to see those who were apostles before I was, but I went immediately into Arabia and later returned to Damascus *(Galatians 1:15–16)*.

My dear children, for whom I am again in the pains of childbirth until Christ is formed in you *(Galatians 4:19)*.

E very man is meant to be the "Bethlehem" of the Son of God by the regenerative power of Redemption. Just as the historic Son of God became Incarnate in the Virgin Mary—"that holy thing which shall be born of thee

264

shall be called the Son of God"—so the Son of God is formed in the life of the individual saint by the supernatural grace of God (Galatians 4:19). Are we willing to submit to the "new man" that is formed in us until our natural life is transfigured by His personal indwelling? It has nothing to do with our eternal salvation; it has everything to do with our temporal value to God. All most of us are concerned about is being saved from hell only and being put right for heaven. But there is something infinitely grander than that. We are given the marvelous chance of giving up our right to ourselves to Jesus Christ so that we may become the devoted bondslaves of God Who saves us so supernaturally.

DECEMBER 26 _____

Christ Breaks In

"Praise be to the Lord, the God of Israel, because he has come and has redeemed his people" *(Luke 1:68)*.

There are those who say there is no such thing as the supernatural incoming of Jesus Christ, either in history or in the human heart. Our Lord Jesus Christ is not Someone Who has sprung from human nature by evolution: He is Someone Who has come crashing into our human nature by the superb miracle of the Incarnation. The supernatural is the only explanation of our lives if we are right with God, and at any moment God may tumble our lives up as He likes. The question is, Are we willing to let Him? We have to maintain our personal relationship to God in Christ Jesus, no matter what happens. The one thing that is of value to God in a human life is a personal relationship of holiness to God, and every part of physical, mental, moral life and of Christian work that is not so related will be desolated and burnt as rubbish.

_____

Dust and Deity

So God created man in his own image, in the image of God he created him; male and female he created them *(Genesis 1:27)*.

And the LORD God formed man from the dust of the ground and breathed into his nostrils the breath of life, and man became a living being *(Genesis 2:7)*.

G enesis 2:7 reveals that man is made up of dust and Divinity. This means that in practical psychology we must always make allowance for the incalculable. You cannot exhaust man's nature by examining his "dust" qualities, nor by describing him in terms of poetic sentiment, for after you have described as much as you can, there is always an incalculable element to be taken into account. There is more than we know; therefore we cannot deal with ourselves as machines. One part of ourselves must be dealt with as a machine, and the more we deal with it as a machine the better; but to try and sum up a man as a machine only is to miss out the bigger part. Or to say that man is altogether a spiritual being without anything mechanical in him is to miss out the incalculable element that cannot be summed up. These two things, dust and Divinity, make up man. "Dust" is man's glory, not his shame; it has been the scene of his shame, but it was designed to be his glory.

_____

The Only True Liberty

"So if the Son sets you free, you will be free indeed"
(John 8:36).

It is for freedom that Christ has set us free. Stand firm,
then, and do not let yourselves be burdened again by a
yoke of slavery *(Galatians 5:1).*

We have to present the liberty of Christ, and we cannot
do it if we are not free ourselves. There is only one
liberty, the liberty of Jesus Christ at work in my conscience
enabling me to do what is right. If we are free with the
liberty wherewith Christ makes us free, slowly and surely
those whom we influence will begin to be free with the
same freedom. Always keep your own life measured by the
standard of Jesus Christ; bow your neck to His yoke alone
and to no other yoke whatever; and see that you never
bind any yoke on others that Jesus Christ Himself does not
place. It takes a long time to get us out of imagining that
unless people see as we do they must be wrong. That is
never Jesus Christ's view. Our true sympathy lies with the
One Who is absolute tenderness, and every now and again
God gives us the chance of being the rugged stuff that He
might be the tender One. We have to be sacramental
elements in the Lord's hands.

_____

Man, After God's Pattern

In him was life, and that life was the light of men *(John
1:4).*

The life appeared; we have seen it and testify to it, and we proclaim to you the eternal life, which was with the Father and has appeared to us *(1 John 1:2)*.

I n Him was life; and the life was the light of men" (John 1:4). Why did Jesus live thirty-three years if all He came to do was to die for sin? He lived thirty-three years because He had to show what a normal man after God's pattern was like. He died that through His death we might have the source of life that was in Him (Romans 5:17). That is why it is so absurd to say, "I accept Jesus as a Teacher only." Try to apply the teachings of Jesus to your life without an understanding of His Death and you will find it cannot be done; it would either make you commit suicide or take you to the Cross and give you an understanding of why it was necessary for Him to die.

DECEMBER 30 _____

Our God, a Consuming Fire

For our God is a consuming fire *(Hebrews 12:29)*.

B ehold, your house is left unto you desolate." Twice before Jesus had said, "My Father's house," the solemn application being that God hands individuals as well as nations over to a desecrated temple which He calls "your house." We need to bear in mind that chaos and wrath are the foundation of the life of every man who does not live in communion with God.

". . . everlasting fire, prepared for the devil and his angels." God's holiness never alters its attitude to devil-ishness; as long as God endures, He endures as "everlasting fire" to the devil. God is "a consuming fire," and if we side with the devil we shall know His burning. Divine fire, as

268

opposed to natural fire, burns the fiercer the farther you get away from it; when you get nearer to God, His burning becomes a comfort.

DECEMBER 31

The Final Vision of the Exalted Lord

Then the eleven disciples went to Galilee, to the mountain where Jesus had told them to go. When they saw him, they worshiped him; but some doubted. Then Jesus came to them and said, "All authority in heaven and on earth has been given to me. Therefore go and make disciples of all nations, baptizing them in the name of the Father and of the Son and of the Holy Spirit, and teaching them to obey everything I have commanded you. And surely I will be with you always, to the very end of the age" *(Matthew 28:16–20).*

By His Ascension Our Lord raises Himself to glory; He becomes omnipotent, omniscient, and omnipresent. All the splendid power, so circumscribed in His earthly life, becomes omnipotence; all the wisdom and insight, so precious but so limited during His life on earth, becomes omniscience; all the unspeakable comfort of the presence of Jesus, so confined to a few in His earthly life, becomes omnipresence; He is with us all the days.

What kind of Lord Jesus have we? Is He the All-powerful God in our present circumstances, in our providential setting? Is He the All-wise God of our thinking and our planning? Is He the Ever-present God, "closer than breathing, nearer than hands or feet"? If He is, we know what it means to "abide under the shadow of the Almighty."